SOCIAL DEVELOPMENT

Conceptual, Methodological and Policy Issues

Edited by
JOHN F. JONES
RAMA S. PANDEY

St. Martin's Press · New York

© John F. Jones and Rama S. Pandey, 1981

All rights reserved. For information, write:
St. Martin's Press, Inc., 175 Fifth Avenue, New York, NY 10010
Printed in India
First published in the United States of America in 1981

ISBN 0-312-73201-5

Library of Congress Cataloging in Publication Data
Main entry under title:

Social development.

   Contents: Introduction to development/John F. Jones
—A unified approach to development/Tarlok Singh—
Strategies for social development/Rama S. Pandey—
[etc.]
   1. Social change—Addresses, essays, lectures.
2. Social policy—Addresses, essays, lectures.
3. Social participation—Addresses, essays, lectures.
4. International cooperation—Addresses, essays,
lectures. I. Pandey, Rama S. II. Jones, John Finbar.
HM101.S6919 1981   303.4   81-4607
ISBN 0-312-73201-5   AACR2

Preface

Social development refers to the process of planned institutional change to bring about a better fit between human needs and aspirations on the one hand and social policies and programs on the other. The concept is a versatile one: it can be used to analyze change at the international level, dwelling on the situation of developing nations, while it is equally valuable as an analytic tool in assessing conditions in highly industrialized countries such as the United States. What makes the concept applicable to a variety of circumstances is the unifying force of the assumption that progress depends not simply on economic growth but also on national efforts which incorporate, in a conscious fashion, social goals. Thus, the quality of life is immediately an issue, since the question cannot be left until the factories have been built before an answer is sought. Likewise, if social development is the ultimate aim of our striving, we will not wait for tomorrow to think about the disadvantaged, the marginal and the alienated of society. A prerequisite for development is the participation of all citizens in building their nation and, simultaneously, in enjoying the benefits of progress. At the strategic level, the solution to human misery must involve an equitable distribution of income, goods, services and opportunities. This does not happen automatically. Citizens have to be involved in seeking the common good. People and plans must be joined. To achieve social development it is necessary that the people play an active role in planning and decision making. Only then is government policy truly public policy.

Social development offers a theoretical framework that allows analysis of diverse social and institutional changes from a unified perspective. The underlying assumption of much of the literature on social development is that the genesis of human problems can be traced to the implementation of various economic and social policies. Pushing the cause back a bit further, the failure of a particular institution—a welfare, health or education program—does not result uniquely from a specific policy but from the very structure of society itself. Thus, when designing a solution to a social problem, a strategy must be devised which can operate on three levels at once. Human needs must be assessed in order to have a sound basis for policy; institutions must be made responsive to the concerns of people; and finally, some structural changes in society may be required to facilitate institutional planning.

The methodology of planning for institutional change involves policy making, programing, administering, organizing and evaluation. Any institutional change requires a policy frame on which to hang goals, priorities and strategies. Programing deals with the problems of designing the service delivery system, setting targets, and making the proper resource allocations. The administrative process should bring about participation of concerned individuals and groups in decision making, organizing aims at preparing people to gain maximum benefit from services and resources, and also to change the system if necessary. Finally, evaluation measures gaps in goals and performance, and provides feedback for further planning.

The book is designed to address these substantive, conceptual and methodological issues in social development. The term 'social development' is rather comprehensive and suggests a holistic approach to the solution of human problems. At the same time, the fact that social development involves linkages with various systems indicates its complexity. By its nature, social development reflects a multidisciplinary orientation. These factors have influenced the organization of the book. Each chapter, as indicated by its title, deals with a core aspect of social development, while allowing a discussion of related issues. Taken together, the chapters give a broad picture of the social development process. All the chapters draw on different sources and illustrations, national and international, to describe development in the hope that the book can offer the reader a blend of experiences.

The ten chapters of the book follow different pathways to the analysis and interpretation of social development. The first four chapters present the conceptual framework of social development. Chapter 1 examines the meaning of social development over the past decades, and the influence it has had (and not had) on national planning. It analyzes the political context of progress. The role of planning and the need for indicators that measure development are also discussed. Chapter 2 elaborates on the relationship between economic, political and welfare institutions, especially with reference to less developed countries. The chapter stresses the diversity in national development experiences, while identifying the components and mechanisms of integrated development. Chapter 3 focusses on such major strategies for social development as income distribution, people's participation, human development, and integration. It discusses the part the institutional context should play in the selection of strategies. Chapter 4 explains the function of international collaboration, multilateral and bilateral, in development. It highlights the role of the United Nations and its member agencies in promoting social development programs. These four chapters present, from an international viewpoint, the conceptual outline of social development.

The next four chapters deal with the methodology of development. Chapter 5 explores the significance of societal values in the formulation of policy. Strategies intended to establish a just social order are suggested—modes of production, organization of work, distribution of rights, and the design of political institutions. Chapter 6 covers program planning. It analyzes the key elements of program planning including social provisions, participation and systematic linkages. Evaluation is described as a feedback mechanism necessary for the correction of program defects and the reformulation of policy. Chapter 7 studies institution building. A vital principle in making institutions responsive to the needs of people is participatory democracy. The Chinese communes and the kibbutzim of Israel are used as illustrations. Chapter 8 examines the strategies of citizen participation. It analyzes the meaning of grassroots involvement, enumerates the obstacles to participation, and finally suggests a partnership embracing professionals and people in the community.

The remaining two chapters deal with education and social development. Chapter 9 takes education in general. It discusses policy issues such as quality, relevance, and the balance to be maintained when striving to ensure that education meets the needs of national development. The chapter discusses problems likely to arise in planning or modifying educational systems. Chapter 10 focusses on professional training. It examines various patterns of social work education designed to prepare practitioners to work in the field of development. Lastly, it outlines a general model of the development process that provides a basis for organizing a curriculum for social development.

The book presents the reflections and perspectives of its ten contributing authors on social development. Although initially designed for use in the curricula, both graduate and undergraduate, of schools of social work and other professions involved in the training of personnel for social development, the book can just as well serve those who are working in the field as policy makers, social planners, administrators, and community developers. We hope that the book will contribute to that body of knowledge which social development education and practice draw upon. It may also stimulate further exploration of social development issues.

Our special thanks go to the contributing authors, all of whom wrote their papers specifically for this book. We are also indebted to the clerical staff of the School of Social Development, the University of Minnesota-Duluth, who typed the manuscript. Finally, we wish to express our appreciation of the Inter-University consortium for Social Development, which sponsored our endeavor.

JOHN F. JONES
RAMA S. PANDEY

Contents

Contributors

JOHN F. JONES is the former Dean of the University of Minnesota-Duluth School of Social Development and currently Professor and Director of Social Work at the Chinese University of Hong Kong. He received his Ph.D. from the University of Minnesota. He has served on several committees on social welfare and development at regional, national, and international levels. He is the author of *Citizens in Service* (with John M. Herrick), and has contributed numerous articles to scholarly journals and periodicals.

TARLOK SINGH was the member of National Planning Commission of India (1950–67) and Deputy Executive Director (Planning), UNICEF (1970–74). He was a Visiting Professor at the Stockholm University Institute for International Economic Studies, Visiting Senior Research Economist at the Princeton University, Woodrow Wilson School for Public and International Affairs, and an Honorary Fellow of the London School of Economics and Political Science. His publications include *Poverty and Social Change*, *The Planning Process*, *Towards an Integrated Society*, and *India's Development Experiences*.

RAMA S. PANDEY, formerly Dean of School of Social Work, Varanasi (India), is Professor of Social Development at the University of Minnesota-Duluth. He received his Ph.D. from Brandeis University. He worked as Program Specialist to the International Association of Schools of Social Work, and as Consultant to United Nations Children's Fund on its global study project on young children. He is the author of *Problems of Social Work Education in India*, and *Child Socialization in Modernization*, and has contributed numerous papers to scholarly journals.

DANIEL SANDERS is Dean of the School, and Director of International Programs at the School of Social Work, University of Hawaii. He received his Ph.D. from the University of Minnesota. He is the author of a book on social security. He has contributed numerous articles and papers to professional journals.

DAVID G. GIL is Professor of Social Policy at Brandeis University. He received his Ph.D. from the University of Pennsylvania. He is the author of *Unravelling Social Policy*, *Violence Against Children*, and *Challenge of Social Equality*. He has contributed numerous articles to professional and scholarly journals and periodicals.

J. F. X. PAIVA, formerly the Director of School of Social Work in Sri Lanka, and Professor of Social Policy and Planning at the School of Social Work, University of Missouri, is currently Advisor to UN Center in Social Welfare and Development at Manila. He received his Ph.D. from Brandeis University. He worked at the United Nations Division of Social Development in various capacities and authored a research project on manpower for social development. He has participated in several international meetings, and contributed numerous articles to scholarly journals.

SALIMA OMER is a Consultant to United Nations Economic and Social Commission for Asia and the Pacific. She received her Ph.D. from Brandeis University. She worked as Advisor to the Government of Pakistan, Ministry of Information and Broadcasting, and was on the faculty of the School of Social Development, University of Minnesota-Duluth. She has participated in several international meetings and contributed numerous papers to professional journals.

NANCY HOOYMAN is Associate Professor of Community Organization and Development at the School of Social Work, University of Washington. She received her Ph.D. from the University of Michigan. She has contributed numerous papers to professional journals and was on the faculty of the School of Social Development, University of Minnesota-Duluth.

P. D. KULKARNI is Professor of Social Policy and Administration at the Tata Institute of Social Services, Bombay. He was the Advisor to the United Nations Asian Centre for Training/Research in Social Welfare and Development, Manila (Philippines). He worked as Director of Social Welfare to Government of India for several years and later on, as Acting Chief of the Division of Social Development, United Nations Economic and Social Commission for Asia and the Pacific. He has participated as an expert in numerous international conferences on social welfare and development and contributed several papers to scholarly journals and periodicals. Kulkarni was also Associate Professor at the University of Minnesota-Duluth School of Social Development.

C. DAVID HOLLISTER is Professor of Social Development at the University of Minnesota-Duluth. He received his Ph.D. from the University of Michigan in Sociology and Social Work. He has been a faculty member at the University of California, Berkeley, the University of Wisconsin-Milwaukee, and Acting Dean, School of Social Development at the University of Minnesota. He is the co-editor of the book, *Community Corrections: A Reader*. He has presented several papers at professional conferences and contributed numerous articles to scholarly journals in the areas of social development, organizational analysis, and criminal justice.

JOHN F. JONES

1 An Introduction to Social Development

AN INTERNATIONAL PERSPECTIVE

THE PRESENT TREND

The urgency of development has led many to a declaration
of war on poverty, ignorance and oppression. The war analogy,
though natural, is ironical, since the one prerequisite of social
development is peace and to borrow metaphors from the military
arena is to play with paradox. The crisis is real enough. The
polarization which has taken place since World War II is global
in scope. At issue is the survival not just of one group or another
but of a world order. The danger of nuclear conflict, mass
starvation or epidemic is quite factual, and the fall-out of any such
event, if it occurred, would not easily lend itself to containment.
Some viruses can be isolated, some conflicts localized. Not all
diseases. Not all wars.

On the world scene, the struggle for survival has been variously
described as a struggle between the haves and have-nots, the
Communist and non-Communist countries, the Northern and
Southern hemispheres, the developed and underdeveloped regions.
The categories overlap and do not take account of fragmentation
within the groups. Furthermore, even by naming the protagonists
in this fashion there is a temptation to see answers to world problems
in purely ideological or possibly military terms. The politics of resentment no less than the politics of power are bound to fail in a
world which requires more than political solutions.

If success in development cannot be guaranteed by political

settlement, neither is it attained through *economic means alone*. The first efforts of the United Nations to promote development were along economic lines, and the policy proved inadequate. In the early 1960s the United Nations launched its First Development Decade, setting a minimum target of 5 percent annual growth—later raised to 6 percent—for the 'lesser developed countries'. Underlying the goal was the hope that the poorer countries would translate their economic progress into better living conditions for all their people. The results of the First Development Decade were discouraging. Despite some moderate economic growth, very large segments of the poorer countries, from 40 to 70 percent, continued to live in utter poverty. The situation was—and is—most grim in countries like India, Pakistan, Bangladesh, Ethiopia, Chad and Haiti, which must provide for growing populations without plentiful resources or strong, industrial economies. Today there are 900 million people living on incomes of less than U.S. $ 75 a year. Simply to set Gross National Product targets without at the same time establishing mechanisms for redistribution frustrates the ultimate goal of development—a higher standard of living for a total population.

In 1970, with many of the first decade's plans still unfulfilled, the United Nations changed its strategy. The aims of development were spelled out in the Preamble of the International Development Strategy for the Second United Nations Development Decade:

> As the ultimate purpose of development is to provide increasing opportunities to all people for a better life, it is essential to bring about a more equitable distribution of income and wealth for promoting both social justice and efficiency of production, to raise substantially the level of employment, to achieve a greater degree of income security and to expand and improve facilities for education, health, nutrition, housing and social welfare, and to safeguard the environment. Thus, qualitative and structural changes in the society must go hand-in-hand with rapid economic growth, and existing disparities—regional, sectoral and social—should be substantially reduced. These objectives are both determining factors and end-results of development; they should therefore be viewed as integrated parts of the same dynamic process, and would require a unified approach. . . .

That social justice, and specifically the elimination of poverty, was the goal of the Second Development Decade was made more explicit in further resolutions. In 1972 a resolution of the Economic and Social Council (1727, LIII) on the 'Elimination of mass poverty and unemployment' recommended to governments of developing countries that:

> . . . within the framework of their national priorities and plans, they define the magnitude and causes of poverty and unemployment prevailing in their economies and prepare action programs, laying down national development strategies to eradicate these conditions.

The recommendation of the Council that the United Nations system gives priority in research and action programs to problems of mass poverty and unemployment was endorsed by the General Assembly in December 1972.

The shift of emphasis to social development was not, however, intended to suggest a dichotomy between 'social' and 'economic' development. Social development refers to the process of planned institutional change to bring about a better correspondence between human needs, on the one hand, and social policies and programs on the other. The words are a shorthand way of stressing the social aspects of development based on the United Nations' definition of the term, namely, '. . . the greater capacity of the social system, social structure, institutions, services and policy to utilize resources to generate favorable changes in levels of living, interpreted in the broad sense as related to accepted social values and a better distribution of income, wealth and opportunities.'[1]

This broad definition of *social development* should counter the notion that development is primarily the concern of *developing* nations alone. All countries without exception are developing. No nation, no matter how affluent, uses its manpower and resources to the benefit of its total population. Another way of putting it is to say that every nation has problems of socioeconomic *under-development*.[2] Furthermore, as the energy crisis has demonstrated, development is not simply a national or regional issue; its implications are worldwide. Because of markets as well as the varied sources of agricultural and industrial production, a nation's wealth is tied to the development of other regions. But advocacy for international development rests on more threatening assumptions than the requirements of good trade relations. The Club of Rome's cry of doom has found listeners not because of computerized prophecy so much as the simplicity of the argument:

> If the present growth trends in world population, industrialization, pollution, food production, and resource depletion continue unchanged, the limits to growth on this planet will be reached sometime within the next one hundred years. The most probable result will be a rather sudden and uncontrollable decline in both population and industrial capacity.[3]

STATES OF CONSCIOUSNESS: GROWTH OF AN IDEA

Concern with development predates, of course, the Club of Rome and the United Nations. The progress of the industrial revolution in the nineteenth century gave Western communities no choice but to confront a novel and, in some respects, frightening technology. It forced an attempt to reshape industrial society to take account of those most affected by the changes, the workers— the men, women and children who labored in factories and mines— or those who, worse still, could find no employment and consequently no place in the new order. That is half the story, the matter-over-mind explanation where people react to a universe of things—machines, factory conditions, scarcity. The other half, bearing on the psychology of development, is no less important. Alongside, even preceding, the industrial revolution went a social revolution which changed the structure of English society first, then that of the Western world. This complex movement—which we might call the social-industrial revolution—required motivation. Those who, a century or two ago, built bridges, dug canals, invented or operated machines did so for a variety of reasons—at times and with some it was motivation to innovate, to automate a craft; at other times it was the desire to reduce physical labor, to make money, to share in increased opportunity, even to expand the common good. Machines followed a wish to invent just as an urge to escape the poverty and oppressiveness of the countryside must have preceded migration to the city. Industrialization depends upon the will to industrialize and it demands some consensus on the part of manufacturers, consumers, technicians, shopkeepers, bankers and workers.

A similar conglomeration of motivating factors is evident in the social-industrial revolution we inherit today. The 'Made in Japan', 'Made in China', 'Made in the U.S.A.' labels on fabrics, toys and machines speak both of survival needs and yearnings. They denote consensus—an agreement within a nation to make things, and between nations to trade. But as the prize is enormous so too the price that has been paid. The rush for natural resources has been responsible for the rape of defenseless societies and of the land itself. The international economic system upon which trade depends has its own inequities that, if left unchanged, would keep some regions dependent upon and subservient to others. The goal of higher living standards and the means to attain this end have not been made available to all. Privileged elites within societies have often cornered prosperity while the very poor remain untouched by the wealth the rich enjoy.

There is a similar case to be made against elite nations; the facts of foreign aid blunt but do not invalidate criticism. The United Nations Conference on Trade and Development, UNCTAD, has had as its goal an annual transfer of ·7 percent of G.N.P. from 'First World' states to developing nations in the form of grants or low-interest loans. This goal the advanced industrial nations have accepted in principle. In the mid-1960s the foreign aid of these countries reached ·44 percent of their combined G.N.P., but more recently it has shrunk to ·33 percent. Foreign aid has undoubtedly contributed to more than 5·5 percent annual increase of the G.N.P. of less developed countries during the last decade, but this percentage of 5·5 is an average figure. Countries such as Taiwan, South Korea and Brazil have prospered above this level, while others have fallen below, and a few, e.g., Southern Yemen and Niger, have actually logged a negative rate of growth. Overall global prosperity, if demonstrated, would hardly console those countries which have no share in it—the likes of Chad, Ethiopia or Bangladesh.

The excesses of economic expansion on the national and international stage have often been justified in the past on the grounds that wealth filters down. Wealth breeds wealth; luxuries become necessities, thus expanding markets and creating opportunities for others. In this view squalor, disease and unemployment are relatively insignificant because temporary; they will wither away with the new state of prosperity. But such a philosophy, in its purest form at any rate, has not withstood time and would find few defenders today. Already in the nineteenth century the State was recognized to have the right and duty to protect workers from the worst effects of industrial growth.

Altruism was not the sole reason for abandoning the doctrine of *laissez-faire*. The consequences of poverty such as malnutrition, illiteracy and chronic dependency as well as the unrest to which oppression gave birth were seen as detrimental to industrialization. During the first part of this century attention was focussed on the obstacles to economic development. Social scientists began to examine the demographic, institutional, structural, religious and psychological factors impeding industrial progress. Familial and kinship structures were scrutinized; economic institutions—ownership of property, land tenure, the shared means of production, saving incentives—were studied, as well as social stratification, role definitions, achievement and award systems in the hope that they would reveal what obstructed or promoted entrepreneurship. Behind the effort lay the assumption that the social structure and value orientation of the West explained its high level of economic development. The goal was economic; only the means—subordinate to the end—were social. Closely resembling this line of reasoning was the theory, promoted after World War II, that in order to create conditions favorable to industrialization a social investment was required, involving human instead of monetary capital. Offensive as the concept may sound, it at least promoted in planning the consideration of social programs in health, housing, education and labor.

The social component of development came in clearer focus with the advocacy of 'balanced social and economic development.' The phrase, summarizing a school of thought, in no sense implied that equal resources should be spent on the economic and social sectors but it did suggest that an optimum relationship could exist between them and that their goals were compatible. The next logical step was the recognition of development as a single, unifying process. The United Nations and its member organizations have promoted the view that the developmental process is a complex whole, comprising economic, social, political and administrative elements. An integrated approach demands that any strategic design for development, whether national or international, has to cover these elements if it is to be effective.

Societal attitudes towards development span a continuum where at one end we find the espousal of economic goals first and foremost and, at the other, national policy committed to integrated development. Industrializing nations nowadays have tended in their public utterances at least not only to favor welfare programs but to stress social justice as the end and object of planning. Thus, the fourth development plan of Iran (1968–72), for instance, in listing its development objectives mentions 'the more equitable distribution of income by providing employment, extending social and welfare services to all, expanding local development and rehabilitation activity, especially in rural areas.'[4] Where national plans reveal their ambiguity is in the failure to state clearly how the aim of human betterment can be achieved. Concrete strategy sometimes inclines to favor economic plans over social goals. Occasionally the dissonance is recognized for what it is—conflicting aims—as in the Third Five-Year Plan of Pakistan where it is stated: 'Conflicts of objectives are inevitable in any plan which runs the entire gamut of the social and economic life of a country; their reconciliation is always a delicate and difficult task. These objectives, only some of which can be defined in quantitative terms, are not necessarily compatible. It is to rapid growth that the nation must look to free itself from poverty, disease, ignorance and inequalities. . . . However, the growth already achieved and that which can confidently be predicted now makes it possible . . . to give greater weight to the requirements of social and economic justice without sacrifice of essential growth.'[5] The words are brave, barely touching on the final difficulty of all development—scarcity of resources.

DEVELOPMENT OBJECTIVES

Since economic growth is a necessary but insufficient cause of development it follows that the other conditions of progress must also receive attention. When social objectives are written into development plans they can serve as a conscience and can guide the economic pace and pattern of a country. Indeed, integrated national policy requires that social dimensions be explicitly considered.

At the heart of social development is the preeminence of human resources. The word can easily be misunderstood to mean that the human element is no more than a resource in development—a manpower supply for industrialization. The concept of human resource development is wider than that of manpower planning and it embraces every measure for the promotion of human welfare. Manpower planning is useful only if it is in accordance with the needs of a nation's men, women and children. Human development is of prime importance and must dictate policy in agriculture, industry and education. When this mandate is recognized, then planning—especially cross-sectoral planning—can best serve national policy in endeavoring to ensure the balanced composition of the population in terms of age and sex; to encourage an even distribution of human resources in various parts of the country and among developmental sectors; to promote the improvement in the attitudes, knowledge and skill of the potential and actual labor force; to improve housing along with the other civic amenities; to strengthen the family and the community and to prepare children and youth for their role as builders; and to provide social welfare facilities to foster and conserve the full potential of every individual to become a useful citizen.[6]

Human resource development requires national population policies. Uncontrolled population growth unmatched by a production increase inevitably spells poverty. Statistics of projected population in Asia alone up to the year 2000 reveal a problem of no small account. A comparison with 1975 population estimates shows that population is expected to double in Indonesia, Iran, Pakistan, the Philippines and Thailand. An increase between 75 and 100 percent is expected to occur in Afghanistan, Bangladesh, Burma, Cambodia, India, Laos, Malaysia and Nepal.[7] Such gross projections do not tell the whole story and should be supplemented by statistics on total population and density of population, population by age, life expectancy, birth rates, mortality rates, and population by sex and rural-urban residence. But projected population statistics serve at least as a warning flag and as an indication of an unsolved problem. The fragile balance of production and population is illustrated by Egypt's Aswan Dam. The dam added 25 percent to the nation's arable land, but in the interval between the planning of the project in 1955 and its completion in 1970, the population of the country grew 50 percent, to more than 30 million.

But national population policies are dangerous if they simply aim at the limitation of population growth without attention to environmental and social conditions. Neo-Malthusians have argued that the world has hungry people because it has too many people. The contention is superficially appealing until it stumbles over the fact that only 44 percent of the world's arable land is being tilled.[8] The question arises, then, why countries do not feed themselves? Unfortunately, in many regions the most fertile land is concentrated in a few hands. Not only is land ownership too often the monopoly of the wealthy and the politically favored, but the largest holdings—according to the World Bank—produce the least food for domestic consumption. What the soil is made to produce are cash crops for export—cotton, flowers, rubber, tea, coffee, bananas, sugar, peanuts, barley. These are largely plantation crops, the capital for which is supplied by agri-business corporations, sometimes multinational or foreign corporations.

With the best land set aside for export crops, the bulk of the population in underdeveloped countries and the rural poor of developed nations is pushed on to the least desirable, the least productive acreage. Most of the Third World people—an average of 80 percent in Asia—are dependent on the land for a living. Paradoxically, it is these very people who are hungry.[9]

In developing countries alternative ways of tackling the problem of hunger include land tenure reform, national policies relating to food production and export, international cooperation, family planning programs, and so on. None of these means is sufficient by itself, and the alternatives are not mutually exclusive. On the contrary, it is necessary to employ a multitude of measures to ensure that the food system operates for the benefit of the poor and hungry.[10]

Failure to come to terms with population growth has accelerated rural-urban problems. Frequently the urban complex becomes the exploiter of a rural hinterland, draining it of skilled manpower while gobbling up its natural resources. Planners have put much of their effort into fostering urban industry rather than integrated regional development. In Asia, for instance, the haphazard growth of the urban population has reached close to 400 million people— nearly double that of the entire United States' population. At the same time, the overwhelming proportion of the Asian population still resides in the countryside and is likely to continue doing so.

Attention to the needs of rural areas has been uneven. Vast areas of Africa are suitable for livestock ranching but require money to eliminate diseases that attack man and beast alike. Strategies for rural development have lacked the follow-through which alone guarantees success, and the strategies themselves have too often been marked by insufficient thoughtfulness. Land reform, even where it has received the sanction of legislation, has frequently failed to become reality just as the miracle seed of the Green Revolution has so far been most useful to the large farmer and the agro-corporation. In poor countries, small landowners need low-cost credit, technical help and a market not upset by excessive food subsidies from donor nations. The countryside is both pro-ducer and consumer—it must feed the nation (at a profit) and be able to consume the goods produced by developing industries. Its needs for full employment are no less than the city's. Labor-intensive manufacturing—cottage industry as well as the factory—should be located in rural areas. The aim of regional development is to achieve a symbiosis between urban and rural areas so that the development of each is complementary to the other.

Since development is for people, a fundamental condition of progress is popular participation. One of the dangers inherent in economic expansion is a widening gap between the traditional and modern sectors of the economy—very often approximating to the agricultural and industrial sectors. Planned regional development can prevent some of this, but to be most successful the planning should involve the participation of the people affected by social change. Popular participation can help reduce the disparities re-sulting from the uneven development of different sections of a country. The principle of community partnership is also appro-priate for the purpose of organizing programs for isolated and dis-advantaged groups such as tribal communities, displaced persons or minorities.

Writers on social welfare generally follow Wilensky and Lebeaux in defining the term to include those formally organized and socially sponsored institutions, agencies and programs which function to maintain or improve the economic conditions, health or interper-sonal competence of some parts or all of a population.[11] They generally follow them, too, in dividing social service programs into residual and institutional with the implication that societies which provide universal benefits are best. It should not be forgotten, however, that in many societies and in many parts of the world social services are a device for redistributing income and wealth and for balancing inequalities. Thus, even in the early stages of industrialization, they are essential for social progress and cannot be postponed till some later date.[12]

Despite the ambivalence with which emerging nations view foreign aid, financial and technical assistance are essential to development. Part of the fear, justified or not, of commercial colonialism can be offset by channeling a greater portion of financial assistance through international agencies such as the World Bank which is already a major source of development funds. Agencies of this type can provide fiscal supervision of projects, discourage prestige schemes that add nothing to the common welfare, and also parry criticism that aid is politically motivated. Apart from financial assistance, there is need for technical cooperation. The transfer of technology is in no way confined to the miracle seeds of the Green Revolution but can take the form of steel-tipped ploughs and improved irrigation.

The Political Context of Progress

Because it is possible to enumerate social development objectives, it should be relatively simple to devise programs to meet the objectives. But between scheme and substance there is a chasm. Planning is one thing; implementation another. Commenting on major programs of rural development in Asia, C. Inayatullah lays most of the blame for their ineffectiveness on the fact that they are intended to be instruments of achieving goals other than those of social justice, and are instead geared to raising agricultural productivity (for some), controlling political discontent and winning support for national elites.[13] According to Inayatullah, the major programs of rural development in Asia can be placed in three main categories:

1. programs intended to alter property relations in favor of the less privileged, such as land reform, which may be called *equality-oriented* programs;
2. programs intended to spread new technology, such as agricultural extension, which may be called *technology-oriented programs*;

3. programs intended to raise community solidarity by fostering new groups and institutions such as cooperatives, local government and community-development. These may be called *solidarity-oriented programs.*

In theory, the programs should work for the benefit of all the people. In fact, they do not. With few exceptions, land reform in Asia has had little effect on poverty. For reasons having more to do with the politics of productivity than social justice, most Asian countries attempting land reform have redistributed land only among cultivators who own farm equipment and bullocks. Left out are the farm laborers and artisans, resulting in division between two poor classes—the landless and the small farmers. Land reform has been further emasculated through half-hearted implementation. Ambiguities in the law, the cost of legal recourse, conflict of interests involving government officials owning land, bureaucratic corruption and the lack of enforcement mechanisms have all helped keep unjust social structures intact.[14]

The aim of technology-oriented programs has generally been agricultural productivity to meet food shortages, feed the cities at low prices, achieve national self-sufficiency in food, and in a few countries earn foreign exchange. In rural areas the most likely to benefit from the new technology are those who can afford it—the large farmers. The least likely to gain are the rural poor, especially agricultural laborers.[15]

The solidarity-oriented programs have been used mainly for political ends—to regulate local conflict and control discontent—and seldom to eliminate exploitation or change the rural social structure. The original purpose of cooperatives, for instance, may have been to do away with injustices in production and marketing, but the cooperative movement has been absorbed by traditional hierarchies and on occasion has even been turned against the poor. Money lenders have been known to borrow from cooperatives to lend to non-members at exorbitant rates and better off peasants have borrowed in the same fashion to buy land from the poorest. Those who are relatively affluent and better educated are in the strongest position to gain control of the cooperatives.[16] And the caste and kinship structure in many places has aided the upper rural elite to hold on to power.

The rural power structure in Asia is changing, admittedly, though not to any great degree in favor of the poor. Rather, the traditional aristocracy is becoming modernized and absorbing into its ranks emerging entrepreneurial groups. Politically and economically motivated, the new elites view community projects and local governments as their own. Central governments could of course counter the influence of the local elites by assisting the landless, the inarticulate and the poor, but governments usually calculate the costs and benefits of intervention very carefully. So the technology-oriented and solidarity-oriented programs fall to the elites because they have the skill to organize, the resources to produce and the political power to frustrate attempts to topple them. As Inayatullah has stated, the pressure on central governments to raise agricultural production in the shortest possible time is generated by several forces—the need to provide food for the politically articulate urban middle and lower-middle classes, the need to cut down food imports to save on scarce foreign exchange, or even the desire to gain foreign exchange through food exports.[17]

What is true of rural power structures in Asia applies by analogy to situations in other places—development takes place not in a vacuum but in a political context. Governments work through local groups and are susceptible to pressure whether by rural elites, urban intellectuals, students, party members or business interests. Political pressure is a reality factor upon which the success of social development depends, and where the masses are ignorant and inarticulate, their concerns are likely to be ignored.

The Planning Imperative

Were logic to rule the world, development would be a rationally planned and executed process. It is not. But the more rational the planning the greater chance it has of reaching a desirable conclusion. Unplanned growth would result precisely in the dreaded state of affairs forecast by Robert Heilbroner in *An Inquiry into the Human Prospect*. Heilbroner writes, '...we cannot reconcile the requirements for a lengthy continuation of the present rate of industrialization of the globe with the capacity of existing resources or the fragile biosphere to permit or to tolerate the effects of that industrialization. Nor is it easy to foresee a willing acquiescence of humankind, individually or through its existing social organizations, in the alterations of lifeways that foresight would dictate. If then, by the question "Is there hope for man?" we ask whether it is possible to meet the challenges of the future without the payment of a fearful price, the answer must be: No, there is no hope.'[18]

The first, most obvious price to be paid is a commitment to reason. Due to the complexity of development issues, only conscious planning makes it possible to put the jigsaw together. A jigsaw which is national has as its pieces provinces, states, cities and counties; an international jigsaw is formed from regions and countries. Central planning is essential because of interdependence, although the way in which planning proceeds will vary with political systems. Paradoxically, the greater the reliance on national planning, the stronger the emphasis will have to be on establishing mechanisms for decentralization also, for local conditions never duplicate circumstances elsewhere. The key to effective government is co-operation—not merely in plan implementation but in planning itself.[19] Some tension in the body politic is bound to exist, given local preference and the demands of strong government. When, however, the split is so pronounced as to suggest a dichotomy, the situation is ruinous for all. Central governments have little to gain from weakened and ineffective subunits while localities only aware of their own identity may end with identity but nothing else.

Central planning is, unfortunately, quite compatible with tunnel vision. In part, the cause of this lies in the origins of planning—policy determines its direction. If policy favors sectoral planning, then sectoral planning it will be. At present planning tends to be almost exclusively sectoral. Planning, at its most general level, is economic, physical and social; but more commonly it concerns itself with smaller categories such as transportation, housing, industrial development of a certain kind, or income security. Consequently most of the social planners are at the sectoral program level and their preoccupation is with program planning rather than broad social policy. When it comes to balancing social against economic concerns, there is usually no single body to speak on behalf of the social services in general. There are of course departments dealing with health or housing or education or welfare and, to the extent that they are their own advocates and exert pressure on behalf of their programs, they influence the allocation of funds for the social sector. But because of fragmentation the advocacy is weaker than need be. In the ultimate analysis, the allocations for social services are determined on the basis of the priorities set by the policy-makers.[20] Integration at the level of the social service sector as a whole would seem to be necessary during a transitional phase before more integrated, socioeconomic planning can be achieved.

SOCIAL INDICATORS

The road to integrated development needs milestones to mark the distance travelled. Otherwise planning is a futile exercise with no way of determining when its goal has been reached. Reliance on economic indicators, such as G.N.P. and per capita income, is insufficient when evaluating development. Other indicators able to discern the social nuances of progress must supplement these aggregative indexes. In the past, ease of choice has to some extent governed the selection of indicators: those indicators most readily identified and available to the statistician received primary attention, even though they failed to measure significant outcomes of national planning—urban and rural employment, change in levels of living, social mobility, the altered status of women, popular participation or the actual exclusion of some groups from economic and social progress. Those who have put their faith in criteria which lend themselves to quantification have tended to assume that quality is a constant factor and that quantitative expansion automatically ensures a desired qualitative level. There has also been a tendency to assume that variables such as economic prosperity and social progress go hand in hand, without analyzing in depth the indicators of prosperity and progress. The social conditions of farmers and workers in the United States during the first quarter of this century failed to reflect the prosperity of the American economy. Today in the U.S.S.R. economic and industrial development is certainly on a par with other Western countries, yet the social situation of its workers— compared with workers in the United States and Western Europe— is poor.[21] It may well be that a unitary indicator portraying the totality of development is impossible to invent, but the measurement of the various components of development is a possible dream.

The United Nation's Research Institute for Social Development (UNRISD) has pioneered in the field of social indicators. Among its accomplishments has been the establishment of a data bank of development indicators for research purposes. Its researchers have attempted to work out those indicators which so far have remained rather elusive: indicators of distribution, especially income distribution; indicators of qualitative factors, such as quality of education; and indicators of environmental conditions.[22] In the study of quantitative analysis in socioeconomic development, the institute's researchers have aimed at refining techniques that can be employed, in the context of a unified approach to development, for determining regularities in the relations of variables, helping to identify patterns of development in individual countries and their changes over time, providing a basis for typological analysis, and assisting in cross-sectoral diagnosis.[23] While it is possible to make a fair guess at conditions necessary for progress, it is exceedingly difficult to point out the actual causes of development with any degree of precision.

The task of measurement becomes even more complex when exploring socioeconomic development at the local level. UNRISD is of course predominantly concerned with the needs for information of planners and policy makers at the national level and is less interested in highly specific information lacking comparability and significance outside the locality, although useful for local authorities. The study of real (as distinct from monetary) progress at the local level can, however, provide a basis for a better picture of social development as it takes place in emerging countries. The hypothesis is that through the systematic examination and mapping of real progress in specific villages, small towns and city districts, it should be feasible to assess more accurately—in a manner national surveys cannot—not only the social aspects of change but the interrelationship of the economic and social factors of development. Systematic information derived at the local level can supplement other sources of information—such as census data, national sample surveys, various special inquiries and administrative files of one sort or another—which at the moment most governments use to assess progress. Those who advocate the collection of 'indicators in real terms' do so on the grounds that these are generally more amenable to collecting and reporting than are indicators of income and expenditure which have their own problems of definition, validation and evaluation. Since the argument may be countered by asserting that in the present state of developing countries the impartial collection of such indicators is almost impossible, we are left either with a choice of two defective sets of indicators or with attempting to combine the sets. Theoretically, the use of indicators in real terms at the local level could flush out significant details that macro-level surveys miss. A major deficiency of national planning has been the failure of national planning offices to obtain adequate information on what is actually happening in the country outside the capital city, what changes are taking place in the villages and towns, who benefits from development, who loses, and so on.[24] Locality studies can reveal flaws in planning and suggest strategies for improvement.

SUMMARY

The changing ideology of development is reflected in the aims of two 'decades' canonized by the United Nations—the first stressing economic growth, the second social development. Even a cliché like social development takes time and effort to invent. In the West, the industrial revolution made the goals of social development a political necessity. Definitions came later, the creation of terms coinciding with states of consciousness regarding development. The developing nations either discovered these insights on their own or adopted the formulations of the West as they moved almost ritually through the different stages: emphasis on economic expansion, awareness of the social obstacles to development, emphasis on social investment for development, emphasis on balanced social and economic development, and lastly, emphasis on integrated development.

As people and planners move away from a dollars and cents view of development, other objectives relating more particularly to the social situation gain prominence. The most obvious of these objectives is human resource development which is a catch-all phrase implying balanced population, the even distribution of goods and services—including education—for the purpose of allowing all people to advance, and a sense of community. The other development objectives are corollaries or derivatives of human resource development—population policy, rural-urban symbiosis (regional development), popular participation, and the like.

When Daniel Moynihan chronicled the fortunes of the Family Assistance Plan under the Nixon Administration and called the tale *The Politics of a Guaranteed Income*,[25] he was presenting a case history of social transition and underscoring a universal point: development is political. In Asia land reform, agricultural extension and cooperatives illustrate the same truth and point to the need for aggressive popular involvement in government. But there is another element without which social development is unlikely to take place, and that is planning. Development is not simply unmindful liberation. The choice of individuals renders chaos possible. The countervailing force to anarchy is national intent. Whether through collective decision or single authority, a population decides upon, consents to or suffers public policy. Policy becomes effective by means of planning.

The ability to measure is crucial for effectiveness. What appeals superficially in economic models is the ease with which economists can set up criteria to evaluate goal achievement. Social development must remain ambiguous and therefore less attractive to many while we await the discovery and/or acceptance of indicators to mark progress. Perhaps acceptance is more relevant than discovery, since at least some of the tools are at hand—crude but serviceable— capable of documenting the social profits and losses of society.

TARLOK SINGH

2 A Unified Approach to Development

Developed social and economic systems have come to be characterized by high and rising levels of per capita income and living
standards, comprehensive systems of social security and welfare,
advanced infrastructures and productive capacities, a network of
public and voluntary institutions, and a growing concern with
the quality of life. The imbalances which persist, to which the
national communities become ever more sensitive, are in nature
marginal rather than fundamental and all pervasive.[1] Through
evolution towards a welfare state or progress towards a socialist
society, developed countries have succeeded in attaining the
substance of what has been sometimes described as the unified
approach to development. The different components of development—social, economic and, in many societies, the political also—
can be seen as functioning interdependent parts of an organic
structure of activities, services and institutions. Therefore, the plea
currently made—unhappily less in national than in international
discussions—in favor of a unified approach to development has
most significance for the national economies and societies of the less
developed countries. What are the limitations and possibilities of
this concept?

COMPLEMENTARY ECONOMIC AND SOCIAL DEVELOPMENT

The argument that economic and social objectives should
be pursued together so that they supplement and reinforce one
another has gained strength from the limited results and the

distortions which have marked economic planning in most of the less developed countries of Asia, Africa, and Latin America. In the past, national plans, when being formulated, presented both economic and social goals. In practice, even within their resource constraints, these plans were heavily biased towards economic growth and the expansion of industrial capacities and infrastructures. Planners underestimated the significance of agriculture and the rural sector and failed to assign a central role to employment and the efficient use of available human resources. On this account and because of current economic pressures and the urgent claims of economic and industrial projects, education, health and other social services lagged far behind the modest targets set in the plans. These tendencies were found to be endemic rather than transitional and, even after a considerable period of development, disparities between economic and social development continued to increase. Thus, most of the less developed countries were in fact confronted by the prospect of an internal social crisis—all the more acute because of population pressure. A few countries saw this crisis as imminent, for others it loomed on the horizon. Could a unified approach to social development, using the expression in its broader meaning, help remove the arrears of the past, or secure more even development for the future?

At the present stage of development, the notion of a unified approach is certainly a persuasive hypothesis. However, we have to admit that evidence of practical success which can be readily cited in its support is still scanty. Not enough has been done in most countries to give a sufficiently concrete shape to the idea. Under these circumstances, the unified approach to development is to be viewed as a proposition demanding not necessarily immediate acceptance but objective examination. The aspects to be considered include the underlying assumptions of the unified approach, the model of development suggested by them, the conditions under which various developmental factors may be combined so as to offer the greatest chance of success, and the issues of policy and planning to which satisfactory answers have to be found, according to its situation, by each national society. This chapter attempts a preliminary formulation of these questions.

ACKNOWLEDGING DIVERSITY

In examining the unified approach to development, it is necessary, first, to recognize the extraordinary diversity in the economic, social and political circumstances of countries in the less developed world. Among the major factors marking out countries from one another are the existing levels of income, the size and pressure of population, the degree to which modern productive capacities and economic and social services have been established, the levels of science and technology, the availability of research and training facilities, the extent to which possession of critical natural resources or favorable location may facilitate export-oriented development, and the ready availability of external resources and know-how. The same notions of appropriate development strategies can scarcely be applied to situations differing as widely as those of populous countries of the Indian subcontinent, relatively advanced countries like the Philippines and Colombia, countries with the developmental lags of Ethiopia, Tanzania or Mali in Africa, or of Bolivia or Haiti in Latin America, and favored locations like Hong Kong or Singapore. As a consequence of economic progress over the past two decades, the range of differences in development both within and between the less developed countries has been further enlarged. Therefore, all general ideas concerning the method and priorities of development must be judged with caution and applied with much variation in detail to the specific conditions of different countries and even of different regions.

Going beyond the vast differences in needs and circumstances which can be readily observed, the unified approach implies a view of development and the development process which is internally consistent. Its emphasis is on long-term rather than on short-term goals. It recognizes that progress towards any specified long-term objectives is subject to breaks and interruptions for a variety of causes. However, the very awareness of lags gives to these objectives a certain vitality and persistence, and they remain closely interrelated. Though some political systems and situations are better adapted than others to ensure continuity and mass support in giving effect to the unified approach, the main concepts are to be interpreted primarily in economic and social terms.

ECONOMIC OBSTACLES

In seeking to cross the barrier of poverty and underdevelopment, the first obstacles are nearly always economic in nature. They include—to mention only the most apparent—the lack of productive capacities and infrastructures, lack of skills and widespread prevalence of low levels of productivity, extreme dependence on agriculture and the simpler forms of production and services, accompanied by underemployment and much waste of human resources, and finally, insufficient capacity to save and to raise the capital and foreign exchange resources needed. Is it surprising, then, that the economic requirements should become the dominant determinant in every country of the strategy of development in the earlier phases? The unified approach to development concedes the role of the economic factor. However, it seeks to bring about a feasible combination of the economic and noneconomic and especially the social and institutional factors in the development process, such as could secure simultaneous growth in output and expansion in the requisite social capacities.

PLANNING AND HARMONIZATION OF OBJECTIVES

The unified approach looks to planning as a necessary tool both for analysis and for the making of policy. Without a systematic diagnosis of the inherent features of a society and its economic needs and problems, there can scarcely be a unified strategy for change. Planning involves an appraisal of various social, economic and political factors in development and of their mutual relationships within whatever the current and accepted constitutional framework may be. These relationships are then projected into the future. In viewing needs and resources at different levels, planning becomes a studied effort to identify key problems, to set standards in terms of the well-being of the population as a whole, and to propose the selection and phasing of public and private investments, as far as possible, on the basis of rational criteria. Among the attributes which may give special meaning to planning as part of the political process are its ability to provide a long-term design of economic and social change, an underlying continuity in approach, objective evaluation, and a readiness to experiment. In separating the long-term from the short-term and the continuing and permanent considerations from those of passing interest, planning aims constantly at reducing the costs and enhancing the gains of development.

The elements to be brought into harmony, progressively over a period of years, may be summed up as economic growth, expansion of economic capacity and utilization of manpower, social and institutional change, balanced social development, and integration between the modern and the unorganized sectors of the national economy.[2] These elements interact with one another at every step. Each element derives its significance from the extent to which it contributes to and is, in turn, supported by a well-conceived design of society and its economic and other institutions. At whichever point we may begin we are led on, step by step, to the other parts of the totality which constitutes a condition of mature development.

Economic growth, achieved cumulatively and with the minimum interruption, is an indispensable requirement for social advance. However, different paths to economic growth will involve differing costs, benefits and time spans, and may have varying consequences for the pattern of social development and impact on different social and economic groups.

It is well to remember that in the earlier stages of planning, when there is little authentic experience to draw upon, it is by no means easy to make clear-cut choices of the paths to be followed. Much development planning is in the nature of responses to immediate problems and adjustments to changing pressures and expectations within the country and to developments abroad. However, in the experience of many less developed countries, decisions on issues such as the following have been critical in determining the pace and pattern of development and the social effects on different sections of the population:

1. the priority given in the scheme of development to agriculture and the rural sector;
2. the relative place assigned to heavy and basic industries, to light industry, to small-scale industry, and to the dispersal of economic activity;
3. the extent to which structural and institutional changes,

especially modifications in the pattern of land ownership and management, form an integral part of the scheme of agricultural development;

4. the role assigned to employment and the productive utilization of human resources, especially rural manpower;

5. the extent to which external resources are drawn upon for the development of the economy and the influence exerted by external aid on a country's own priorities and pattern of development.

TURNING POINT FOR THE UNIFIED APPROACH

As stated earlier, in the first phases of development, planners generally put insufficient emphasis on agriculture, on human resources, and on the social aspects of development, while industry and the related infrastructures claimed much the greater part of the available resources. Under these circumstances, the search for a more unified approach would have required, first and foremost, a definitive change in national priorities. Judging by actual resource allocations in several countries—of which India can serve as an illustration—the development of modern industrial capacities and infrastructures was taken to be the key to long-run economic growth. There was an element of truth in this belief, given the conditions of a country such as India. However, even there, the costs of development greatly increased when insufficient attention was given to the linkages between different periods, so that each phase of growth and development failed to prepare the ground systematically for the next, resulting in serious gaps and imbalances. As a consequence, the social benefits of development were pushed into the future to an extent that has not been adequately appreciated.

A second error in development planning was to give too narrow a meaning to the concept of 'economic capacity'. This was taken to mean primarily the capacity to produce modern, sophisticated industrial machinery, where a broader interpretation could have given the term considerably more social content. Growth of economic capacity includes not only the ability to produce in industry as well as agriculture, and the capacity to save, to export, and to pay for imports, but also the capacity to provide work and livelihood for the entire working force of a nation. Once employment and the effective use of human resources become organic to the idea of growth and development in economic capacity, measures for the improvement of health, education and welfare and for raising the general level of productivity find their right place in the scheme of things. This, then, is the critical point of change from the customary outlook on economic growth to the unified approach to economic and social development. The provision of work opportunities and planned and constructive use of human resources constitute a prime condition equally for economic and for social development. Where and so long as this priority is weak, political declarations to the contrary notwithstanding, the social gains from development cannot but be disappointing.

Economic and Social Dualism

In varying measure, the great majority of the less developed countries present a picture of economic and social dualism. On the economic side, there is the marked contrast in income and productivity between those engaged in the modern sectors of activity and the vast numbers subsisting in agriculture, rural labor, small industry and trade. Social dualism is reflected in wide-ranging differences in living conditions, educational levels, and health standards, and in the extent to which the essential social services are available to different groups in society.

Traditional forms of social stratification—such as are implicit, for instance, in caste, in feudal land and labor relations, and in inherited differences of wealth and income—are greatly accentuated as new forms of production and services and new ways of generating income begin to emerge.

Neither economic nor social dualism can be brought under control, much less diminished, without a serious effort to bring about a new relationship between the organized and the unorganized sectors of the economy. This means that, in addition to institutional support, measures of structural reorganization have to be undertaken, such as will enable economic units like farmers, artisans, laborers and small entrepreneurs, who now remain weak and dispersed, to pool together for an increasing range of operations. To the extent to which this change can be brought about successfully, they will be able to engage in their existing activities and enter into new fields with greater profit and on more nearly equal terms. In turn, they will share more adequately in the benefits of growth, the widening of markets and the increase of productivity.

A Model of Development

In the model of development visualized in the unified approach, economic development is to be achieved to the maximum extent possible through policies, programs and activities that simultaneously enlarge social potentials and bring about social development as a necessary consequence. Here, social development is viewed as embodying not only a range of social services and benefits but also changes within the social fabric affecting property, production, and human and social relationships. Such a comprehensive approach will not be possible without certain political and civic conditions. A unified approach demands national policy and direction, local community responsibility, and the involvement of individuals in their own welfare and in the welfare of those nearest to them. A variety of political forms and institutions could provide for these conditions more or less satisfactorily, so that it is unnecessary to identify the unified approach rigidly with any one type of political institutions or model of political development.[3] What could be said perhaps is that a unified approach is a product, in the last analysis, of a model of development whose economic, social and political features are in essential harmony with one another. If the political factor is not congenial, we can scarcely expect the degree of continuous impact and dynamic citizen cooperation in implementation without which the desired economic and social gains will not be sustained.

Components of the Unified Approach

In addition to the commitment to provide work for all and to put the available human resources to the fullest use, the unified approach to social development may be said to have the following main components:

1. equitable distribution of income and wealth and the establishment of conditions of equal opportunity;
2. provision of adequate educational opportunities for the entire community, including children of school age, children and

youth out of school, and adult men and women;
3. provision of health, nutrition, and family planning and welfare services, especially for the rural population and the poorer urban groups;
4. provision, by stages, of social assistance and security systems;
5. establishment of favorable conditions for the development of children, adolescents and youth;
6. measures for the accelerated development of the weaker and relatively nonintegrated groups in society.

These different elements in the unified approach are mutually supportive of one another. They represent continuing priorities, though, in given phases of development, some elements may have to be given greater support than others. Every economic system faces constraints on resources and personnel, the effectiveness of methods and institutions has to be reassessed from time to time, and new problems may demand concentrated attention. In the experience of many countries, the building up of a sizeable network of social services has been a long-term undertaking spread over twenty to thirty years and even longer. There are marked gaps to be filled even when fairly advanced stages of development are reached; meanwhile, new needs will have taken shape. The existence of social gaps and emergence of new needs are important reasons for giving to local communities and institutions a fundamental role in implementing and developing social services of direct concern to the people. Local communities can also take the lead in strengthening delivery systems and in bringing various services and benefits within reach of the weaker and the more disadvantaged groups.

MECHANISMS FOR INTEGRATION

The gains from the adoption of a unified approach to social development depend largely on the extent to which various social measures are planned and operated in a system which is capable of adapting to changing needs. Therefore, it is necessary to distinguish the unified approach, considered as a general design or blueprint for development, from the specific steps which are taken from time to time to implement a total plan. Selectivity and phasing are essential here. Resources can be dispersed too widely all at once, ignoring the strategic points in development. Every political system is subject to popular and party pressures to take a short view and to embark upon over-ambitious schemes and projects which have little relation to one another.

The unified approach to social development is likely to bring the greatest benefits when there is some social mechanism and administrative device for giving a sense of common purpose and direction to diverse activities. The nature of the integrating mechanism may differ from country to country and from one phase of development to another. The point can be illustrated by a few examples. In India, the planned expansion of the rural health services has come under the umbrella of the community development program. As a modest core of community services came to be established in a large proportion of development blocks, progressively, the concept of integrated area development has provided the dynamics of change and coordination. In Tanzania, health, education and water supply services in the rural areas are being built more and more around *ujamaa* or communal settlements and joint farming. In China, communes have been the focal point for the organization of rural health services and other social programs. The programs are organized on the basis of local resources and responsibility, but come within the general framework of national and provincial plans for development. In the U.S.S.R. collectives and state farms have become natural units for organizing programs of immediate concern to the population, including preschool education, health education, and medical services. In many countries, and with varying efficiency, urban centers, municipal institutions, neighborhood councils, factory towns and housing settlements have provided the social base for integrating different services.

In spreading the benefits of social development, the remoter rural areas and the poorer sections of the urban population are almost always the last to be reached. Therefore, the concept of a unified approach must be able also to draw upon a powerful social and political impulse that insists on due care for the needs of the weaker groups and the have-nots of society and on assuring a state of equal opportunity within each community. In other words, the search for a unified approach must be accompanied by a sharp break from traditional values and social stratification and a determination to evolve better integrated and essentially equal communities. Structural reorganization in agriculture, far-reaching changes in administrative systems, and extension of the economic role of the State facilitate the expansion of social services, but these latter fulfill their purposes truly only when there is deep and pervasive concern for the well-being of every member of the community.

The total national environment may favor the adoption of a unified approach to development, especially in its social aspects. For instance, the desire for development and modernization may well take the form of social movements in support of national unity and integration. More specifically, these movements may stress measures for carrying health education and welfare services to those sections of the population who were neglected in the past. From a different standpoint, in the socialist countries, fundamental alterations in property relationships and in the social basis of production helped bring about those conditions of equality and social change to which a unified approach to development in its social dimensions became a natural sequel.

ENLARGING OPPORTUNITIES FOR INTEGRATION

Opportunities for integrating economic and social development are especially favorable where (a) priority has been given to activities which call for such integration; and (b) measures have been introduced with a view to assuring a common minimum of amenities and services for the entire population.

Integrated economic and social development can be expected to yield its greatest benefit under two sets of conditions, namely, where economic and social conditions are highly conducive to rapid growth, and, secondly, where there are large lags to be made up as speedily as possible. Irrigated areas, agricultural tracts where rapid technological changes have been stimulated—as under the impact of high-yielding varieties of cereals—and regions within the immediate influence of large industrial projects are examples of situations in which growth may be accelerated by the adoption of integrated strategies. On the other hand, backward areas and sections of the population handicapped by poverty, illiteracy and ill-health illustrate situations in which only combined economic and social programs, supported adequately by political action, will lead to significant change. In cities and towns in all less developed countries, the problems of those living in slums and shantytowns and in poor neighborhoods have been greatly accentuated by rapid increase in population and rural-urban migration and the inability of civic authorities to meet growing needs. These problems can be approached with some hope of success only with a combination of economic and social strategies. In a number of countries there are large nomadic groups that have remained cut off from the mainstream of development. The economic and social needs of such groups have to be approached simultaneously both through new opportunities for training and employment and through the improvement of housing settlements, health, education, nutrition and other services.

The pursuit of a national minimum calls for the coordination of several forms of action. A national minimum is both an economic and a social concept. Unless a minimum level of income can be assured to all groups in the population—essentially by providing work opportunities and raising levels of productivity—large numbers will be unable to benefit from the available social services. Without an unquestioned priority in favor of social and human resource development, a fair share in resources is unlikely to be allocated for the building up of education, health, welfare and other services. Even with considerable progress in social services, groups in greatest need must still be identified and delivery systems adapted to their circumstances. A national minimum can be hoped for only when

1. the economic investments are designed to lift the economic levels of the population as a whole and especially of those most likely to be left out of productive opportunities;
2. the social investments are calculated to strengthen the human and the social base and thereby give greater meaning and vitality to economic growth.

Thus, in moving towards a national minimum, economic development and social transformation operate as a single, interpenetrating strategy.

SOCIAL CHANGE AND THE UNIFIED APPROACH

As suggested already, in the less developed countries the elimination of mass poverty and establishment of effective equality of opportunity are possible only through economic growth, social progress, and political action. In defining the means by which the unified approach to social development may be advanced, the specific characteristics of each national society, its institutions, its patterns of development in the past, and its resource limitations are the main determinants. In pursuit of social development, the sequence in which different steps may be taken will inevitably differ from one country to another, and generally applicable strategies can only be stated in the broadest terms. There are, however, two factors which, although they may vary with circumstances, will play an inevitable role in development: institutional change and the priority given social investment.

In countries with long established feudal traditions or other differences in caste, class or opportunity, far-reaching social changes and changes in property relations are an indispensable phase in the transition to a modern society. These changes may be said to influence the development of society in a manner analogous to the effects of a 'big push' in relation to the economy. In particular, they induce and even force changes in attitudes and in human relations in the direction of equality. Political systems which are committed to radical social change within the framework of legislative consent, supported by public opinion, may be able to move to the unified approach with greater smoothness than those resorting, by choice or necessity, to violent change.

PRIORITIES IN SOCIAL INVESTMENTS

Whatever the circumstances in which radical social changes occur, the careful planning and phasing of social investments, so as to minimize costs and maximize benefits, is a necessary condition of effective social development. The details of priorities have to be determined by each society according to its resources and other factors. Every nation, whether by design or omission, makes its social investments, and there are few countries which do not offer examples of imbalance—where, for instance, a costly commitment to urban industrialization has been at the expense of the rural population or where public health has taken second place to productivity. The elitist bias of national policy makers has all too often dominated the early phases of social development. However, some useful lessons can also be drawn from past experience. Investments devoted to children and mothers have wide-ranging spread effects and can also generate considerable support from local communities.

In the work of UNICEF and WHO since the early fifties, rural water supplies and relatively simple measures for improving the nutrition of children and mothers have emerged as basic priorities. At the regional level within each country, the more backward areas have required longer periods of preparation than the more advanced areas. Therefore, there has been need for considerable variation in detail to meet regional and local requirements.

As we move from objectives to means, the unified approach to social development resolves itself into a series of related strategies concerned with phasing and priorities within each distinct service and across different social programs. They will relate to urban and rural conditions, to the more backward regions, to the poorer groups in the rural population, and to slum-dwellers and the poorer neighborhoods in cities and towns.

RAMA S. PANDEY

3 Strategies for Social Development

AN ANALYTICAL APPROACH

The concept of social strategy plays a significant role in guiding decisions and actions for achieving social development goals. However, the concept, like other key concepts in social development, requires refinement in its meaning, scope, and application. In this chapter an attempt is made to develop a conceptual framework for identifying and analyzing strategies for social development. It will draw much from development planning where this concept is used in dealing with economic policies and programs. Furthermore, the development thinking and experiences at the international level provide a rich source of information. The focus will be on strategic questions and issues encountered in the field of social development in more developed as well as less developed countries.

PARAMETERS

Social development is generally characterized by a multiplicity of goals and priorities, a diversity of resources, and a variety of institutional linkages. These may be identified as the parameters of social development strategies. The goals in this context are stated as improvement in the quality of life of the people; promotion of economic growth through human resource development; equitable distribution of income, resources, and benefits of development; broad-based participation of people in the process of development and related decision making; and special measures that will enable marginal groups and communities to move in the mainstream of development.[1] The priorities are generally assigned to weak and vulnerable groups in the population, such as the rural and urban poor, ethnic minorities, youth, women and children, and backward communities and regions.

The concept of resources for social development is defined in a broad sense and includes measures that are fiscal, human, and institutional. The fiscal resources indicate what proportions of national income and public outlays are allocated on human services; how this amount is distributed over different sectors such as health, housing, education, and so on; and what the role of the private sector is in the development of human services. The human resources refer to the health status of various population groups and provisions for different levels of education and manpower training. The institutional resources include the network of organizations and delivery of human services that are protective, preventive, curative and rehabilitative. The institutional linkages most critical to social development are those between levels of planning, such as local, regional, and national; between sectors of development such as economic, political and social (and within the social sector between social services such as health, housing, education, and welfare); and finally between time horizons, such as short-term, medium-term, and long-term.

These components of social development provide the framework for identifying social strategies and analyzing their operative contexts. That is to say, a strategic approach requires an analysis of its interactions and impacts at all levels: goals and priorities, resource availability, and institutional linkages.

STYLE OF SOCIAL DEVELOPMENT

The key components of social development tend to be interrelated parts of a growing and evolving system. Each of them is subject to planning and change, and thereby effects changes in other components. For example, any change in goals and priorities may have implications for the allocation of resources and institutional linkages, reflecting a certain style of social development.[2] The style may vary from one country to another. In a particular country, social development may be characterized by its emphasis on top down, bureaucratic approaches to dealing with human needs and community problems. The development efforts and resources, however, may be directed toward changing the existing style into a preferred style of social development. The latter orientation might give high priority to local community development and stimulate a variety of community based social programs and services. Any such changes require a development analysis and strategic thinking. The objective of a social development strategy in this context is to translate a preferred style of development into concrete choices and priorities, specifying the resource allocations, instruments, and institutional changes.[3] In a concrete situation, of course, a social development strategy is always guided by existing conditions and by factors that are both internal and external. Its viability and effectiveness will vary with countries and with stages of development in a country. Whatever is socially and economically feasible and desirable at a particular stage of development may in future no longer be so, or may acquire different dimensions.[4]

SOCIAL STRATEGY AS A CONCEPT

Social strategy has been used rather loosely in the analysis of planned social and institutional change, reflecting such diverse sources as military science and game theory. It would be useful to give here the precise meaning and dimensions of the concept for analytical purposes. Social strategy is generally defined as 'a settled course of action judged most appropriate to achieve specific social goals. It involves broad directions and instrumental approaches; specifics and details of these approaches are discussed as tactics.'[5] Recent advances in game theory have further refined the concept and identified certain new dimensions. According to this theory, a strategic approach takes into account the anticipated responses and decisions of supporters, parallels, and adversaries. The outcome depends on the assessment of those 'moves in their interdependence.'[6] Game theory suggests 'a simultaneous performance of many actors and institutions, a progression over time phases, and a notion of means-ends chain, where all of the simultaneous performances are at once ends in themselves, and means to a more general end.'[7]

The analysis of multiplier effects is another dimension of social strategy. These are defined as the wide ranging impacts of a social intervention. In a society faced with acute problems of low resources and poor health conditions it seems, essential to follow an approach that would focus intensively on certain critical activities, areas or social groups. However, a socioeconomic diagnosis is necessary to indicate the areas for action and the measures most likely to have an impact across development sectors.[8] The purpose of this diagnostic analysis is to identify, generate, and exploit complementarities and feedbacks, and to avoid contradictions or negative side effects.[9]

The impact of social strategy might be viewed from another perspective. A particular strategy may be functional to certain social development goals and target systems, but it may also produce certain dysfunctional effects on target and nontarget systems. Similarly, the impact may be felt at more than one level. In many social contexts, it is difficult to identify and assess the full range and depth of strategic effects. A strategic approach is designed to produce certain primary effects, but its secondary and tertiary effects also need to be identified in the development process because in a particular context these often generate more critical issues for social development.[10]

Major Social Development Strategies

A grasp of the parameters, styles, and the concept of social strategy is useful for identifying different strategies for social development. The major strategies for social development are identified as income distribution, popular participation, human development, and social integration. These are identified as separate strategies for analytical purposes. In a specific situation, one could find a dominant strategy or a mix of selective strategies that were adopted to achieve social development goals. The following section will analyze these strategies according to their tasks, roles, instruments and outcomes.

I. DISTRIBUTIVE STRATEGY

The distributive strategy is geared toward achieving social equity in the process of national development. It includes equitable distribution of income, resources, and wealth. It may also include equal access to employment opportunities, consumption goods, and social services. Any such strategic approach might require more or less simultaneous changes at three levels: the distribution pattern of current income, the structure of wealth resources, and the distribution of future benefits accruing from development programs.

However, the development setting, level, and experiences of a particular country might make one action more feasible and acceptable than another. A distributional diagnosis should specify the expected impact of different component measures of a strategy on different population groups. It might probe such basic questions as 'who pays? who distributes? who benefits? on what conditions? and in what ways?'[11] Such diagnosis could also establish the minima or norms of distribution and determine the extent to which they might be realized in any specific contexts.[12]

There are several factors that influence the trends and outcome of a distributive strategy. They include the characteristics and distribution of power in society, the political commitment to social development, the structure of the economy including control over the means of production, and consumers' demands for goods and services.[13] Each factor plays a critical role in shaping the strategic measure. For example, the question of income distribution is most closely associated with the distribution of power. In Latin America, and that also applies to other developing regions, policies adopted are effective in redistributing income within the middle strata and contribute to improving the relative position of some organized urban groups, but have little effect on the general distinctions between upper, middle and lower strata.[14]

A distributive strategy may comprise a variety of institutional measures to achieve the goals of social development. These are generally identified under three broad categories: fiscal, occupational, and social welfare. Fiscal measures used as instruments of the distributive strategy are geared toward raising public revenue and distributing the burden of taxation more equitably among broad income groups. Different taxation measures are recommended as appropriate to different social strata. The occupational measures are related to wage payments and different kinds of benefits that are associated with the work input of an individual. Both fiscal and occupational measures, according to Titmus, 'can have major redistributive effects in terms of command-over-resources-through-time by certain social groups in the population.'[15] The social welfare measures are designed to redistribute social resources for meeting those basic human needs which could not otherwise be met even at the minimal level through the institutions of the family and the private market.

Thus a distributive strategy requires social analysis and

simultaneous action in several directions: income, wealth, goods and services; social classes and institutions; and instruments and measures. Distributive strategies at the international level are generally geared toward the poorer strata of society, access to consumption goods and social services, broadening the base of public social action, progressive financing within the public sector, and productivity. These are some general strategic issues that must be analyzed in the process of social development planning. However, one might also observe considerable variations in different national contexts.

II. PARTICIPATIVE STRATEGY

One of the major goals of social development is to effect structural and institutional reforms in order to involve all sections of the population in the development process, leaving none outside the scope of change and development. There are three distinct but closely related aspects of this process: mass sharing of the benefits; mass contribution; and mass involvement in the decision making process. While the two-way relationship between mass contribution to development and mass sharing of its benefits has long been recognized, popular participation in decision making is a relatively new concept. Recent national experiences suggest that various social development goals require broad participation of the masses in the decision making process.[16] Here a link is considered essential between the 'development through whom' and the 'development for whom' concepts at all levels of decision making: local, regional, state, and national.

A participative strategy may address itself to such specific questions as: who is to participate? why? through what channels? and in what kinds of programs?[17] It may focus attention on the potential role of the large population strata characterized by low income, low educational levels, and restricted or nonexistent opportunities. In the case of less developed countries, the participation of youth and women is most critical in the process of social development.

The primary focus of participative strategy is on changing the role and character of the government in relation to social development. In almost all countries, the government has already assumed responsibility for social and economic change but is under the influence of elite classes. In these situations, a participative strategy might be directed toward changing the administration's elite class character into a government of and by the masses.[18] This means broadening the scope of public social action and infusing it with citizens' input. The process involves recognition of conflicting interests, but it stresses their constructive handling with a view to achieving some sort of consensus. Thus, the strategy demands continual interplay of initiatives from above and below, along with an interplay of conflict and consensus at many levels of the social order.

Lack of adequate institutional support is a constraint on effective participation in social development. Many countries have developed a network of popular institutions at the local level, but they do not provide for any institutional channels for citizens' input at higher level policy making and planning. Frequently people have been mobilized around certain development issues and activities, but they have been unable to sustain their efforts. Sometimes their energies are misdirected to certain channels that might be dysfunctional to the process of social development. Hence, it is widely held that mass mobilization in order to sustain development requires popular institutions at different levels.

III. HUMAN DEVELOPMENT STRATEGY

The people are involved in social development in several capacities: as resources, agents, and beneficiaries.[19] Development planners have for a long time viewed the people merely as a resource. Their thinking was based on a false distinction between capital investments which promote economic growth and social expenditures which divert resources from economic growth. The human resource approach, on the other hand, lays stress on the enhancement of productivity and on the income generating capacity of the labor force. Human beings play the roles of agent and beneficiary, not merely of resource. They contribute values and preferences, participate in the implementation of policies and programs, and share the benefits of national development. This broad perspective has led to the redefining of social development as an investment in human beings, aimed at improving the condition and quality of human life. Thus social development planning focusses on total human development including productive capacity, participatory skills, and cultural experiences, and on the development of all sections of the population. It is also directed toward enhancing the capacities and opportunities of the present generation without diminishing the potential of future generations.

The human resource approach to social development is also linked with the concept of human rights. A United Nations report, referred to earlier, which examined the human resource approach in the light of human rights, found the two notions complementary. Each calls for the universal provision of social services and the development of specialized services to realize individual potentialities. The report concluded that the human resource approach concentrates on the general supply of qualified persons to fill the occupational, social, and political roles that are essential to the functioning of modern urban-industrial societies. 'It does not place equalization of social opportunities in the foreground. It is quite possible that in a condition of extremely uneven and concentrated modernization and income distribution, the human resource approach could coincide with the continuing marginalization of large population strata. Thus the question of human resource development cannot be separated from the general question of rights, opportunities, and general human well-being.'[20]

The conflicting orientations in the conception of human development get reflected in the setting of priorities, choice of instruments, and allocation of resources. For example, a social development plan may encounter a policy dilemma between universal primary education and the training of middle-level technicians. Similarly, primary health care and nutritional measures are often juxtaposed with specialized medical and health services. An alternative strategy might combine universal provisions of primary health care and primary education against the development of higher education and specialized medicine. These are illustrations of conflicting orientations in any human development strategy. The fundamental problem of public social policy is to identify the right balance between different strategic measures. Again, the balance will change with changing priorities at different stages of national development.

A human development strategy may address itself to the question of achieving the broad goals of social development. It may be geared toward enhancing the capacities of all sections of the population and promoting the multiple roles of producer, consumer, citizen and family member. The strategy requires universal provision of social services such as education, health, housing, nutrition, vocational training, and recreation. Universality may be combined with special social provisions to meet the needs of weak and vulnerable groups in society. Positively discriminating policies define selective services as a social right based on the needs of specific, disadvantaged categories, groups, and territorial areas. The amount, range and quality of social services along with questions of accountability and access are other issues that pertain to the human development strategy. In a specific context, these issues are largely defined according to the stage of national development reached, social priorities, cultural preferences, and political commitment to a particular concept of social development. It is usually assumed that the level of social services corresponds to the level of national income or the income of certain sectors or regions. Furthermore, increases in the social services are proportionate to increases in the national income. An analysis of many national development plans would seem to confirm these assumptions.[21]

IV. SOCIAL INTEGRATION STRATEGY

Social development is also characterized by an integrative approach aimed at bringing isolated and peripheral groups, communities and regions into the main stream of national development.[22] In any country there are numerous social groups—ethnic, tribal, caste, and occupational—and various regional communities which do not feel identified with the development priorities of the larger society. They cannot participate in and share the benefits of social and economic development unless special measures and institutional arrangements are adopted to break their isolation and build up their capability for effective participation in decision and action. The problems of such groups tend to be circular, and special planning for them requires a package of mutually supportive measures.[23]

An integrative strategy might be directed toward reducing or eliminating any disparities between different regions, social groups or communities. This requires a careful analysis and assessment of the social situation and of the potential impact of a particular social measure on various social groups. In a particular political context, the social development strategy may be geared toward mobilizing resources for one set of social priorities to the neglect of others. For example, many national development plans have given high priority to local community or regional development but have often failed to reflect serious concern for the disadvantaged groups of the population.

Social integration strategies are frequently marked by general conflict. One such strategic conflict is identified in the arena of autonomy vs. integration. Many regions or social groups, however peripheral their place in national space, do not like to lose their self-identity or merge into the larger social system. Special measures adopted to change their status strengthen separate identity and continuation of privileged status. Another strategic conflict could be identified at the level of resource transfer. An integrative strategy often involves transfer of social and economic resources from one region to another region, from affluent to weak and disadvantaged groups. This will have political and social repercussions. Under these conditions, not every social and institutional innovation designed to promote integration will be a viable and acceptable measure. Conflict situations demand a careful social and political diagnosis. Attention to political costs and benefits is inevitable in all national integration strategies, for the achievement of social development goals depends upon the proper selection of means.

THE INSTITUTIONAL CONTEXTS OF STRATEGIC ASSESSMENT

The preceding discussion on four major strategies for social development suggests another dimension for analysis. This is related to the social or institutional contexts of those strategies. One particular strategy might be directed toward dealing with different social sectors such as health, housing, education, and welfare. Another might aim at changing the relationship between different sections of the population or regions of the country. Strategies might involve various levels of government or be employed within distinct time frames. In brief, social strategies operate within specific institutional contexts. No single strategy encompasses the total field of planned institutional change in a country.

At the international level the major contextual variables or dimensions in social development analysis, are identified as cross-sectoral, cross-sectional, cross-spatial, multilevel, and intertemporal.[24] The following table shows the chief analytical contexts of different development strategies. The discussion that follows on specific analytical contexts will explicate the role of different strategies in achieving social development goals.

TABLE: SOCIAL DEVELOPMENT STRATEGIES AND
THEIR INSTITUTIONAL CONTEXTS

Strategies	Institutional Contexts				
	Cross-Sectoral	Cross-Sectional	Cross-Spatial	Multi-level	Inter-temporal
Distributive		X	X		X
Participative	X	X	X	X	
Human Development	X	X	X		X
Social Integration		X	X	X	

I. CROSS-SECTORAL CONTEXT

Social policies and programs are traditionally handled by different ministries or departments of national and state governments such as health, housing, and education. There is no mutually supportive relationship between programs in the different sectors. These sectoral approaches result in inconsistencies and contradictions in the process of development. A particular social goal such as child welfare or health improvement is defined in sectoral terms. The actions relevant to that social goal are scattered among multiple decision centers. Very often the social goal is identified with the limited approaches, instruments, and techniques of a particular ministry. This sectoral approach is not helpful in assessing all the potential resources available for a set of social development goals. It does not deal with the differential impact of a particular strategy on different social sectors and social groups.

The purpose of cross-sectoral analysis in social development strategies is threefold: first, to establish development profiles and identify lagging social sectors along with the leading ones (for example, sectors of possible underinvestment or overinvestment or inefficient investment); secondly, to determine positive or negative linkages across different sectors; and thirdly, to specify the kinds of sectoral activity that have the most desirable implications for multiplier effects. This approach requires that various indicators of social development be identified and their interdependency analyzed. The study of interdependence may reveal how these indicators are related among themselves as input, output, and distribution factors. An analysis along these lines should identify normal patterns of development. It should point out the amount of development in different social sectors (the question of proper proportion) and the kinds of development in relation to each other (the question of proper linkages and responses).

The implications of this analytical approach are important for social development. Very often services like health, education, and social security do not reach low income families, particularly those living in rural areas. A simple descriptive analysis of social sectors might indicate gaps and differences in their investment, priorities, and orientations in terms of both institutions and personnel. A cross-sectoral analysis here may further suggest the need for measures such as decentralization of social services and popular participation in their planning and implementation, education of low income people, training of paraprofessionals, and environmental improvement.

A cross-sectoral approach is especially useful when dealing with diffuse socioeconomic problems, addressing the needs of target areas and groups, evaluating concrete projects, and coordinating information. Certain critical and pervasive problems like environmental pollution must be defined cross-sectorally from the very beginning. A multi-sectoral approach is required so that marginal groups such as the urban or rural poor may move from a situation where they lack opportunity as well as bread to one in which they participate in their own destiny and share in the benefits of development. The evaluation of concrete projects must take into account the whole range of development objectives by exploring the linkages and wider repercussions of projects in addition to their beneficial and harmful consequences for target and nontarget populations. A cross-sectoral approach is also the only effective means of elaborating information systems capable of coming to grips with the complexity of social development.

II. CROSS-SECTIONAL CONTEXT

As stated earlier, social development aims at participatory democracy which involves all sections of the population in the development process. Despite this goal, experience indicates that certain major groups of the population are frequently excluded from the mainstream of socioeconomic development. These include small farmers, farm laborers, the poor in slums and shanty towns, youth and women.

A cross-sectional analysis is useful for identifying what roles, if any, these major groups play in development and the extent to which they are excluded. The purpose of this analysis is not only to identify the differentials in participation but also to understand why the differentials exist and how they can be reduced. An analysis of this sort can point to the need for particular intervention strategies in national development.

Various research techniques may be employed to diagnose the differential rate of participation in the process of development. Some barriers to participation relate to goal formulation, structural constraints and institutional arrangements, and the scope of development activities. Very often social development goals are formulated in a way that all the people do not feel identified with the goals. Structural constraints within the social system or within the process of development are another factor in differential participation. A particular social system may not allow mobility to certain ethnic, caste, or tribal groups. Similarly the use of a particular technology in development may rule out the involvement of one group, say women, in that process. Lack of institutional arrangements might be another impeding factor. The choice of a particular social development activity may also restrict any broad-based participation. For example, a development plan may not provide any program that involves women or aims at improving their status in society. Similarly, a program in rural development might be directed toward helping farmers on the basis of matching contributions. This could rule out any meaningful role for the landless population or the poor farmers. A social development strategy could be designed to deal with one or all of these barriers. It could stipulate a broad framework for goal development. It could be directed toward removing structural constraints and providing institutional arrangements that would facilitate the active participation of all sections of the population.

III. CROSS-SPATIAL CONTEXT

Considerable variations are observed in the levels of social development across regions within a country. Frontier regions and depressed areas very often fail to reach the minimum standards of social development whether in income distribution, educational opportunities, health conditions or popular participation. A cross-spatial analysis is useful for identifying backward regions and communities, diagnosing their social and economic underdevelopment, and assessing their potential for improvement. Such an analysis requires social and economic data along regional lines. An opportunity analysis is needed to assess the cost and benefits of undertaking different development projects. A development profile can indicate the flow of resources and pace of social and institutional changes in these areas. A planner may wish to know to what extent ecological factors are responsible for the low resource base of a particular region and how much the national economy and public policy are contributing to regional poverty.

A social development strategy may address itself to the issues raised from a cross-spatial perspective. Planning may be directed toward correcting economic imbalance and improving social backwardness by overcoming ecological constraints, it may be oriented towards more equitable distribution of national resources, or it may include both approaches. Development poles and development centers possessing both economic and social components also have strategic importance in a cross-spatial context.[25] The development strategy may require some change in the structure of the national economy and in the thrust of public policies contributing to regional disparities. Special measures could prevent the emergence of new backward areas and bring the existing ones into the mainstream of national development.

IV. MULTILEVEL CONTEXT

Social development planning involves more than one level of administration; it requires disaggregation of national goals and priorities at state, county, and city levels. Such planning also implies articulation and aggregation of local and state needs and priorities at the national level.[26] Social policies and programs are too often initiated at the national level, and are administered in a top down manner without regard to the aspirations of local communities. The grassroots approach, so critical to social development, is constrained by two sets of factors. The autonomy of the local community in setting its own goals and priorities is restricted and frequently made meaningless by administrative and financial controls and by guidelines formulated outside the community. There is also a lack of institutional arrangements for making local needs known at higher levels of government. Decentralization at sub-regional and local community levels is one strategy to strengthen the grassroots approach. But if, as happens in so many cases, administrative decentralization does not allow for community participation, its very purpose is frustrated in that control remains within the bureaucracy.

Any achievement of national targets depends upon the co-operation of different levels of government and nongovernment organizations in development planning. A multilevel analysis can identify the weak points in interorganizational linkages, diagnose the cause of weak linkages, and suggest measures to broaden the base of social development without losing national perspective or administrative efficiency. Other factors such as the style of political decision making, patterns of administration, resource planning, or the structure of the economy can also be obstacles to multilevel development planning and must be analyzed when designing strategy.

V. INTERTEMPORAL CONTEXT

Social development planning, like its economic counterpart, operates within certain time frames, generally identified as short-, medium-, and long-term. In most countries national plans define the time horizons, and social planning is expected to conform to the schedule. According to Waterston, the generally preferred duration for medium-term development plans is from three to five years.[27] This is short enough to permit reasonably accurate projections and estimates and long enough to cover the lead time or gestation period of a sufficient number of major projects. However, such medium-term plans need to be supplemented by short-term plans which may be either rolling or annual. Rolling plans imply continual review and revision and demand flexibility within the planning process. Annual plans, an alternative to rolling plans, allow some of the same flexibility in that they provide planners with the opportunity on a yearly basis to review medium-term targets and to modify original estimates. Medium-term plans of three to five years also operate best within the framework of a long-term perspective plan. Thus, one visualizes supporting linkages between periods of development planning. A perspective plan, addressing the long-term needs of a nation, sets the stage for medium-term plans, and—within medium-term plans—annual or rolling plans are utilized to decide upon immediate measures for promoting development.

Social programs present the development planner with a major difficulty. Goals such as improving the quality of education, changing the pattern of consumption, raising the standard of living, and adopting family planning practices usually involve structural changes in society and demand longer time spans than are necessary in the economic sphere. To complicate matters further, different social goals and projects require different amounts of time for their gestation and maturation, and for their effects to become visible. Generally, social development plans should be flexible enough to take into account political expediency, analysis of new data, intermediate outcomes, and growth in knowledge and technology. In social development planning we are too often faced with the 'apparent dilemma of a single term plan lumping together social policies and programs needing different time horizons versus a set of short-term, medium-term, and long-term plans without real links.'[28] It is in this context that intertemporal analysis is so important.

The goal of any social development strategy is to promote supportive relationships and minimize conflict in policies and programs. An intertemporal perspective offers a solution to the complex question of complementarities and conflicts in planning. Within a brief time frame, two development targets might appear to be in conflict with each other but, viewed over a medium- or long-term range, they may turn out to be interrelated and mutually supportive. For example, given the scarcity of resources, a short-term perspective might suggest that economic investment targets conflict with targets relating to primary school enrollment and the expansion of health care. But a long-term perspective might suggest otherwise. Social programs may improve the quality of the labor force and increase productivity. An intertemporal analysis could indicate alternative ways in which various social groups or regions of a country might be mobilized to achieve their specific goals while contributing to the development goals of other sectors.

SUMMARY

The four major strategies for social development and their five analytical contexts provide a comprehensive framework for identifying, monitoring, and evaluating institutional and structural change. Most governments recognize the importance of social development in national planning. However, the lack of a clear definition of social strategies makes the full integration of social and economic goals in national plans extremely difficult. The result is that social development frequently forfeits its claim over national resources. Social analysis is a method of clarifying issues, and it should lead, almost as a matter of course, to strategic planning.

DANIEL S. SANDERS

4 International Cooperation for Development

At a time when the urgency of international collaboration to promote development is clear, critical questions are being raised in some advanced nations relating to its feasibility and, indeed, its very purpose.[1] There is a climate of skepticism about programs of aid to less developed countries which borders on disillusionment. This is not an all-pervasive mood, but the lessening of support for cooperative endeavors is evident. It can be explained in part by the pressure which industrialized nations experience to put their own house in order—a demand from within to tackle native problems of poverty, unemployment, urban decay, environmental pollution and energy shortage. Whatever the reason for the coolness towards foreign aid, its consequences are great. The widening gap in productivity and living standards between the rich and the poor nations is a matter affecting social justice and, ultimately, peace.[2] According to recent U.N. reports about 20 percent of the world's population, or one out of five persons in the world today, suffer from absolute poverty. The response of the international community to the challenge of development in the context of world poverty will determine the kind of world society in store for succeeding generations. Indeed, there are those who suggest that the nature of the response will determine whether or not there is a future for man.

THE OBJECTIVES OF COLLABORATION

Any discussion of international cooperation must elaborate on its major goal or objective—in this case, social development—but it should suffice at this point to sum up the more obvious characteristics of social development and then differentiate between primary objectives and objectives that are instrumental in attaining the overall goals of development. Socioeconomic progress encompasses more than an increase in national output or income, and has as its final goal the capacity of a society to enhance the quality of life for its citizens.[3] It is in this context that Gunnar Myrdal suggests that development is a movement upward of a whole system of interdependent conditions—a system consisting of several categories of causally interrelated conditions of which economic growth is just one.[4] This perspective is no less necessary when considering foreign aid than when addressing a nation's internal policies. International cooperation should strengthen national development plans which must take into account both social and economic factors—in policy formulation, plan implementation and the allocation of resources.[5] In addition to focus on overall rates of economic growth, there is need for emphasis on specific human concerns such as abolition of mass poverty, improvement of employment opportunities and the satisfaction of basic needs of all people at the earliest possible time.

It is evident that the low income countries of the world have opted for social development. This is a piece of their 'unfinished revolution.' The primary objective of the international development effort must then be in keeping with these national goals—a long-term, self-sustaining capacity for social progress on the part of low income countries.[6] Side by side with the goal of reducing social and economic disparities within countries goes another primary objective of development—to reduce the gap between rich and poor nations.

Realistically, it may not be possible to close all gaps or remove all inequality, but the progressive reduction of disparities and the lessening of inequities within and between nations is an integral part of the quest for social justice in international relations. Despite the efforts of the United Nations and the activities of two development decades, the gap between rich and poor nations continues to grow. There exist structural inequities—in trade relations, in control over natural resources, in access to technology—that call for concerted efforts based on considerations of social justice. The resolutions of the U.N. General Assembly embodying the program of Action on the Establishment of a New International Economic Order, adopted on May 1, 1974 and the Charter of Economic

Rights and Duties of States adopted on December 12, 1974, have emphasized that what is called for is not just a refurbishing of the old framework of cooperation among countries but a new set of guidelines and relationships based on mutual interest and respect among nations.[7] The demand for greater equity among nations, in addition to being a demand for narrowing gaps in levels of living is also, and perhaps more importantly a demand for a fairer sharing of power and decision making. Increasingly, this emphasis on mutual respect and parity in power, and the related strategy of self-reliance, is responsible for the renewed emphasis on cooperation among developing countries.

In addition to the overall objectives of international cooperation, there are others which are instrumental and carry strategic implications for promoting development. One important instrumental objective is that of free and equitable international trade. The abolition of import duties and excessive taxes levied on primary commodities produced by less developed countries is one specific change that would have a freeing effect on international trade.[8] Some of the other objectives that have strategic relevance for the realization of the principal goals of international development are: the fostering and strengthening of a multinational aid system; an increase in the quantity of foreign aid that is distinct from military aid; a more effective coordination of aid; efforts to deal with the population explosion in developing countries; and support of education and research geared to the needs of developing countries.

It is evident that International assistance for development to be most effective requires a climate of partnership. Such partnership and mutuality does not imply a *laissez-faire* attitude on the part of donor nations or organizations, towards the use to which financial aid is put. Rather it suggests that developing countries are free to move forward in their own way but, where assistance is given, with built-in constraints and monitoring procedures mutually agreed upon.

THE SCOPE OF INTERNATIONAL COLLABORATION

While it is edifying to outline the ideals of development, the real world (in which international cooperation fades or flourishes) has its own order. In international development—as in other areas of human effort—motives tend to be mixed and they influence the objectives as well as the scope of activities. Ideally, international collaboration should focus upon, and bring about, quantitative and qualitative improvements in education, health, welfare, agriculture, housing, banking, transportation, and so on. It should stimulate growth in the diverse sectors of developing nations, speed social equality, and move communities towards distributive justice. But the motivation for requesting and giving aid is variously based upon political, military, strategic and humanitarian considerations. It should come as no surprise, then, to note changing patterns in the scope and outcome of aid activities.

Much of the aid that was given developing countries following World War II was designed to meet emergencies considered political or military in nature. Humanitarian motives tended to be secondary. While not denying the presence of altruism, it is possible to interpret the increase of U.S. foreign aid in Asia during the 1950s mainly as a response to cold war conditions. Even here we can detect elements of a vaguely conceived development program which had the potential of transcending purely strategic imperatives. Myrdal has written of the intellectual duplicity implied in too closely identifying aid programs intended for the benefit of underdeveloped countries with the national interests of the United States. An unhappy consequence of this identification was that when a particular international policy backfired, American disillusionment with foreign aid in general grew.[9]

Acting somewhat as a brake upon purely national interests in development aid, a number of international organizations—particularly the United Nations and its specialized agencies—have focussed on the tackling of many of the urgent social and economic problems, such as food production, health, nutrition, social welfare, population growth, industrialization and employment. In doing so they have provided a stimulus for development among the emerging nations. Initially the focus of aid given by these agencies was on material assistance in times of emergency. But other activities supplemented the instant aid and assumed increasing importance in time—multilateral assistance in national programs, the exchange of technical experts, periodic study conferences and seminars, educational opportunities for people from less developed countries, and the fostering of regional research and training centers. Much, however, remains to be done. The resources available to the respective U.N. agencies for making any significant impact on these problems are limited. There is also the important task of devising new instruments not only for the transfer of technology but in a more important sense for the creation and dissemination of technologies to meet the needs and conditions of the developing countries.

PATTERNS OF COLLABORATION

As we examine collaborative efforts in development, it is clear there are diverse auspices and patterns that have evolved. The extent to which these efforts are effective is to some degree determined by the nature of the auspices and the patterns of collaboration. It is important therefore to find out what patterns of collaboration seem to contribute most to development and to ascertain the reasons for their effectiveness.

Collaboration for development generally has been under the auspices of intergovernmental agencies such as the United Nations, private international organizations such as the World Council of Churches, national public agencies with international interests, and in particular countries, private organizations with a history of international service.[10] The development efforts fostered by the United Nations, the International Bank for Reconstruction and Development and other international agencies has tended to be multilateral in form. In contrast to this the development activity of national public agencies—such as the United States Agency for International Development (USAID)—has generally assumed a bilateral pattern.

Often, the bilateral aid given to less developed countries has been directed toward short-term political gains, strategic advantages or trade benefits for the donor.[11] The desirability of aid programs which reflect narrow national interests is increasingly coming into question. The Commission on International Development has advocated channelling aid through multilateral, intergovernmental organizations such as the U.N. The most important benefit emerging from multilateral cooperation is that it promotes a relationship of mutuality.[12] It restricts the role of narrow national considerations in aid policies, and opens opportunities for recipient countries to monitor donors, for donors in turn to monitor recipients and other donors and to assess performance according to criteria agreeable to the parties concerned.

In the international community, the United States has been

tardy in supporting attempts to implement multilateral and cooperative aid to developing countries in a manner most in keeping with the spirit of the United Nations Charter. Based on national self-interest—as political and strategic considerations seem to dictate—the United States has continued to favor bilateral forms of aid. There has been a tendency, for example, to tie both aid and loan assistance to less developed countries to exports from the United States in order to ensure considerable trade benefits for the donor. It should be pointed out that the United States is not the only 'First World' country resorting to this policy, and that the amount of aid it has given over the years to developing countries (measured in dollars and not percentage of G.N.P.) has been massive.[13] The United States must, however, accept its fair share of blame for setting a pattern followed by other industrialized countries in tieing development aid to narrow national goals. The consequence of this policy—where a set-back in one area can result in a general disillusionment with foreign aid—has been mentioned already. Any change in policy leading to a multilateral pattern of aid, freed from the politics of giving, would affect in a positive manner future international cooperation.

THE ROLE OF THE UNITED NATIONS

The preamble of the United Nations Charter refers to the goal of promoting progress and better standards of living for all people. The United Nations has always been aware of its own responsibility to provide intergovernmental leadership. Its surveys and demonstration projects, the exchange of information and personnel which it has sponsored, and its emphasis on research and training have all stimulated development.

In 1961 a resolution of the United Nations General Assembly launched the First Development Decade. Despite reservations expressed about the relatively limited impact of the first decade, there were some important gains—given the enormity of the task. For example, the average total growth rate of 70 less developed countries showed an annual growth rate in keeping with the 5 percent growth rate projected for the decade and 20 less developed countries logged an annual growth rate of more than 6 percent.[14] Nonetheless, the economic gains did not guarantee social betterment for all nations—or even for all the population of those countries enjoying industrial expansion. The change of strategy marked by the introduction of the Second Development Decade, with its emphasis on a unified approach to development, signified concern with such issues as the population explosion and the need for structural reform within countries to promote progress. The document which sets forth the U.N. policy for the 1970s stated clearly that 'what development implies for developing countries is not simply an increase in productivity, but major transformations in their social and economic structures.'[15]

A landmark in international collaboration for social development was the first United Nations Conference of Ministers Responsible for Social Welfare held in 1968, focussing on the role of social welfare in the context of national development.[16] When discussing the development of human resources, the Conference paid particular attention to the strengthening of family life and the preparation of people, especially children and youth, for social progress. The Conference noted certain areas of strategic importance in which international cooperation might play a role. Technical assistance could enable governments to formulate effective policies at the national level, to determine priorities in resource allocation, and to ensure the integration of policies and programs. Social welfare research under international sponsorship could be of practical benefit to less developed countries. The intergovernmental auspices of such study would not infringe on the freedom of each country to pursue its own solutions in accordance with individual needs, resources and priorities.

The United Nations and its specialized agencies have long been involved in providing technical assistance. The United Nations Research Institute for Social Development in Geneva, for instance, conducts both field surveys and macrostudies on problems of socio-economic development—research that ranges all the way from identifying indicators of social progress in small communities to studying the implications of the large scale introduction of high-yielding varieties of foodgrain, otherwise known as the Green Revolution. The United Nations Children's Fund has the goal of strengthening family life by supporting programs aiding children and youth, through its educational efforts in the area of parenting, and by its attempts to advance the status of women. Technical assistance for family planning is available to developing countries through the U.N. Fund for Population Activities, the World Health

Organization, as well as the UNICEF. Each of the specialized agencies has its goals and programs; and, while some duplication of effort is inevitable, the aim of the United Nations is to coordinate the endeavors of its various units.

One outcome of the United Nations Conference of Ministers Responsible for Social Welfare was the establishment of regional centers for training and research in social welfare and development. The potential of these centers to stimulate development is great in that the research and training are geared to specific geographic areas rather than the world-at-large. An example of regional effort having precise relevance for one area (while still having a more universal application) was the expert group meeting on the Determination of Social Development Content in Social Work Education Curricula, held in Bangkok in 1974, which came to grips with educational and development issues in Asia. International collaboration may have global goals but unless these are stated in regional terms they are less likely to be achieved.

CURRENT REALITIES AND FUTURE DIRECTIONS

No structure such as the United Nations will effect development without substantial support from the world community—a commitment to social justice on the part of governments and peoples of the technologically advanced as well as the emerging nations. Although the purposes of development may seem Utopian—self-sustaining growth where this is lacking, equality among nations, and among citizens shared prosperity and freedom—the international community can only ignore these yearnings at its own risk, for the anguish, frustration and suffering of masses in underdeveloped areas of the world must inevitably threaten peace. In a sense, even the pragmatic approach to international aid, of enlightened self-interest on the part of advanced countries, will point to the urgency of responding to the human misery and poverty experienced by developing countries.

Social progress depends upon success in surmounting obstacles. The barriers in the case of international cooperation are many and strong. The first barrier is apathy—the lack of a widely shared and steady commitment to development. In many of the wealthy countries, development is not yet a central concern for governments, business, labor, youth or individual citizens. National defense, even space exploration, frequently rank higher among priorities. Only an intense educational program aimed at illustrating the consequences of underdevelopment—war, epidemic and famine—will alter attitudes, stir consciences, and lead possibly to a reordering of national goals.

Another barrier to international cooperation, mentioned earlier, is the fact that aid policies are too often dominated by political, military and strategic interests of the donor countries. With the exception of Sweden and a few other small nations, there is very little development aid given solely for humanitarian purposes. In keeping with the philosophy of national self-interest, donor governments favor bilateral patterns of aid so that they retain control of events, and are reluctant to channel resources through intergovernmental agencies such as the United Nations whose multilateral aid can more easily protect the autonomy of recipient countries. Bilateral aid carries with it a tendency to duplicate the assistance programs of other, possibly rival nations. The result is a multiplicity of competing agencies promoting their own projects while remaining inattentive to the efforts of other groups. The rivalry breeds waste and makes it next to impossible to initiate joint monitoring of projects or a review of the general utilization of development assistance.

There are other obstacles to development to be found within the less developed countries themselves, in their institutions and structures, and in the traditional attitudes and practices that prevent socioeconomic progress. Often substantial change is possible only through revolutionary political action. But the political institutions in the countries most in need of social reform are weak and there is limited popular participation. Instead we find special and elitist interests dominant and standing in the way of the common good. These groups resist structural and policy changes in education, agriculture and taxation.

Given the obstacles to international development, what does the future hold? The future relies on the present, and international cooperation is only as strong as the concept of a world community.

What is needed is a new philosophy of development assistance which differs from the old attitudes towards foreign aid based predominantly on national self-interest. Development can no longer be viewed as simply 'growth'—an increase in the G.N.P. of the country as a whole, without special regard to how that increase was achieved, who benefitted at whose expense and what other problems were caused. New approaches to development emphasize the fact that improving the lot of the vast number of people who are poor can best be done, indeed in most cases done only, by attacking their basic problems directly, rather than assuming that they will benefit from overall economic growth.[17] The issue is an international one that goes beyond the boundaries of this or that State, and its international dimensions must be clearly perceived. Myrdal has advocated the common recognition of aid to underdeveloped countries as a collective responsibility of the industrialized nations. The burden of this could be shared in an equitable manner, amounting to a system of international taxation.[18] Here education for a new approach to development aid is necessary to convince governments and people of their obligation to participate in multilateral programs of assistance. The question of labeling is important in this context—aid given for military reason is best called a national defense expenditure and removed from the aid budget. Citizens often take what their governments label foreign aid to mean development assistance when in reality it includes armaments, military training and advising. If military expenditures were severed from the aid budget, it would be possible to establish financial assistance targets and measure achievements in international development apart from strategic or military considerations. What the dollar amount of foreign (nonmilitary) aid ought to be depends, of course, on a number of factors including the state of the world economy and the G.N.P. of particular countries. In 1968 the Swedish Parliament determined that its foreign aid budget should be increased from then on by 25 percent until it reached 1 percent of its G.N.P. in the fiscal year 1974–5. Were this the goal of the rich countries of the West, East and Middle-east, coupled with policies aimed at promoting private investment in countries which badly need foreign capital, then hopes for world progress would be brighter. The risk of trade domination or the fear of exploitation is never entirely absent in aid programs, but both the risk and the fear can be minimized by channeling assistance through international agencies such as the World Bank.

Foreign assistance alone cannot guarantee a new order. In the words of an Egyptian official, 'no nation, no matter how rich, can develop another country.'[19] Developing countries must do a number of things for themselves including initiating fundamental reforms to break loose from the monopolistic controls—especially in education and the ownership of land—that reinforce economic and social inequalities within those countries. Tradition may hinder rather than help here. In education, for instance, custom favors the humanities rather than vocational and technical training. Land reform remains a poor man's dream in many countries; the land measures which might make it a reality have not been taken—clear and precise legislation, favorable terms of credit, improved market outlets, the provision of fertilizers. In Asia and Africa the proclaimed goal of 6 percent annual growth in G.N.P. will not be attained without institutional reforms and attention to regional problems such as population growth. National policies must take into account tradition, custom and belief but these considerations cannot be an excuse for governments refusing to tackle issues relating to agriculture, industry, foreign investment, population size and education. Development depends upon basic reform.

CONCLUSION

The rationale for international collaboration lies in the nature of the development process which is basically a cooperative venture. Even economic expansion rests on an agreement (voluntary or forced) to trade. This is much more the case with social development whose goals embrace the quality of life not of selected groups but of people everywhere. Just as citizen participation forms the bedrock of national development, so participation by diverse cultural groups, by governments, by world organizations is a necessary condition for global survival and betterment. What this betterment is defies simplistic definition. Perhaps it is, in A. N. Whitehead's words, 'the vision of something which stands beyond, behind and within the passing flux of immediate things.' But if the full meaning of the human person remains a mystery, we can at least claim a role in attaining more immediate and manageable objectives relating to equality, liberty and security. Because these are human concerns, they break the boundaries of geography and nationality and are essentially cosmopolitan. In this context it is increasingly clear that, to ensure success in international collaboration for development—in addition to the new philosophy of development, innovative ideas and strategies—what is fundamental, is a new resolve to pursue more vigorously a concerted plan of action that is already being perceived with reasonable clarity.

DAVID G. GIL

5 Social Policies and Social Development

A HUMANISTIC-EGALITARIAN PERSPECTIVE

This essay explores the relationship of social policies and of policy-relevant societal values to social development. Its thesis is that the scope, direction, and quality of the social development process are largely shaped by the social policies and the dominant value positions of societies.

Social scientists and others using the concepts of social policies and social development tend to attach different meanings to them. Hence, it is necessary to begin with an explication of my conception of these terms and of the societal processes to which they refer. Furthermore, since such explications are usually not value-neutral, I will first specify the value position from which my conception derives.

This value position may be summarized as follows: All humans everywhere, despite their manifold differences and their uniqueness as individuals, should be considered of equal intrinsic worth. Hence they should be deemed entitled to equal social, economic, civil and political rights, liberties, and obligations. Societal institutions on local and translocal levels, should assure and facilitate the exercise of these equal rights, and the free, autonomous, and authentic development of all humans. All humans should be considered 'subjects'; none should be treated as 'objects' or 'means'. Hence no human should dominate, control, and exploit other humans.

Socially structured equality should not be interpreted, vulgarly,

Previously published in *The Journal of Sociology and Social Welfare*, Vol. III, No. 3 (January 1976), pp. 242-59.

as arithmetic equality or uniformity. Rather, it is to be understood as a guiding principle to be implemented creatively through flexible institutions, designed to assure to all humans throughout the life-cycle satisfaction of their unique needs, and actualization of their unique individuality, subject to constraints implicit in population size, aggregate wealth, and level of overall development.

SOCIAL POLICIES

Social policies may be thought of as clusters of rules or as insti-tutionalized guiding principles maintaining a social order.[1] These rules and principles evolved throughout the history of human groups. They reflect choices and decisions made by successive generations striving to satisfy basic biological and emerging social and psycho-logical needs as they pursued survival in the context of relative scarcity. Social policies reflect stages in human evolution beyond total dependence on instinctual dynamics and randomness in human behavior and relations. They represent significant steps beyond the trial-and-error stage of the struggle for survival. Social policies are products of the human capacity to reflect on experience and reality and on the existential imperatives encountered by all human groups, to devise systematic answers to these imperatives, and to pass these answers on from generation to generation. Eventually, social policies evolved into patterns or blueprints for societal exis-tence, organization, and continuity.

With time, social policies, like other products of the human mind which are transmitted among generations and experienced in the course of socialization as social reality, tended to take on a life and dynamics of their own, and to exist independently of the humans whose choices created them. Consequently, social policies confront subsequent generations as powerful forces that shape life and reality and that act as constraining influences on the development of new approaches to the solution of existential problems. Their sources are no longer remembered, and the more independence they acquire with time, the more resistant to change they are likely to become. Frequently, they are not even identified as social policies but are referred to as 'customs,' and 'traditions.' Quite often, also, they are viewed as 'laws of nature,' as eternal and inevitable and not subject to critique and change by a present generation.

Yet humans in any generation ought to realize that behind any particular set of social policies are human choices at certain stages of history, choices which produced one possible model for organizing human existence and survival based on insights and knowledge available at the time. The choices made and the patterns resulting from them may not have been the best possible answers even at the time they were made, nor are they necessarily the best pattern for subsequent generations including the present one. Hence, optimally, each generation should claim its right and responsibility to re-examine transmitted social policies in the light of present circumstances and knowledge, and in relation to currently held values which may differ from the value premises underlying past choices.

As for substance, social policies always represent solutions to the following fundamental, existential problems which any human group must resolve in some way:

1. What resources to select for development from the natural environment in order to assure survival and to enhance the quality of life?

2. How to organize the production of goods and services needed for survival and the enhancement of the quality of life; or, more specifically, how to design and maintain a division of labor, including preparation of individuals for, and their allocation to, specific sets of work tasks so as to assure a smooth performance of all the work necessary for generating the goods and services deemed needed by society?

3. How to divide or distribute among members of society the aggregate product of their aggregate labor, the goods and services generated for survival and for the enhancement of the quality of life; and, related to the distribution of concrete goods and services, how to distribute among members of society honor and prestige, civil liberties, and political rights?

As a society develops and, over time, institutionalizes specific solutions to these fundamental, existential issues, it determines indirectly the circumstances of living of every individual member, and of every group. For the circumstances of living of individuals and groups are largely a function of the activities they engage in, or the work roles they perform, the concrete goods and services they receive, and the honor, prestige, civil liberties and political rights they may claim. Furthermore, in shaping the circumstances of living of individuals and groups, social policies also determine the nature and quality of human relations in a society, since reciprocal relations among individuals and groups tend to be a function of their respective roles and rights. Finally, the overall quality of life, or the existential milieu prevailing in a society, is also shaped by its social policies since that quality may be understood as the aggregate of individual circumstances of living, the resulting quality of human relations, and the quality of the environment which in turn results from the interaction of humans with their natural habitat.

Summarizing then, social policies are conceived of here as rules or guiding principles for maintaining a social order, reflecting choices and decisions evolved over time concerning: the selection and development of life-sustaining and enhancing resources from the environment; the division of labor or allocation of work statuses and roles in a society's aggregate system of work and production; and the distribution of goods and services, honor and prestige, civil liberties and political rights. Together, through their interactions, these developmental, allocative, and distributive decisions and processes shape the circumstances of living of individuals and groups, the quality of human relations, and the overall quality of life or the existential milieu of a society.

VALUES

A second concept which requires explication here is that of values. Theodorsons' *Modern Dictionary of Sociology* defines a value as

An abstract, generalized principle of behavior to which the members of a group feel a strong, emotionally toned positive commitment and which provides a standard for judging specific acts and goals....

... they are often regarded as absolute, although the formation and apprehension of values evolve in the normal process of social interaction....[2]

Values may also be thought of as early layers of social policies. Their origin, evolution, and dynamics are nearly identical to those of all social policies. They differ, however, from other social policies in the level of generality and abstraction, and in the extent to which their origin in human choices is no longer realized. The sources of values are frequently projected on to non-human, supernatural powers.

Analysis of the substantive content of many values suggests that they derive from basic choices compatible with the perceived interests of entire societies, and/or the perceived interests of groups who gained influence, power, dominance, and control over the rest of society. Eventually, values evolve into powerful factors legitimizing established interests and maintaining the status quo of social orders which is shaped by these interests. Values are usually guarded and disseminated by priestly and other elites involved in processes of socialization and social control. Over time clusters of related and mutually reinforcing values became integrated into internally coherent ideological systems, which constitute constraints on, and often insurmountable barriers to, the malleability of social policies and social orders. Social policies will generally conform to prevailing ideologies and to particular constructions of social reality implicit in such ideologies and in turn will reinforce the ideologies as decisive forces in society.

VALUE DIMENSIONS RELEVANT TO SOCIAL POLICIES

In studying social policies and their relationship to social development one need not concern oneself with every possible value, but only with value dimensions which are likely to affect developmental, allocative, and distributive decisions, decisions which have been identified in the preceding discussion as the key processes of social policies. Values influencing these key processes may be appropriately referred to as social-policy-relevant value dimensions.

The most significant value dimension from a social policy perspective is that of equality-inequality. In developing resources, a society may assign equal or unequal importance to the needs of all its members and segments. It may design a system of division of labor, and may allocate work roles within that system on the basis of equal or unequal access and assignment. And finally, it may distribute goods and services, honor and prestige, and civil liberties and political rights on equal terms as universal entitlements to all or, in unequal terms, as differential rewards for different role and status clusters, access to which is restricted differentially.

Whether or not a society will employ egalitarian criteria in its developmental, allocative, and distributional decisions will depend on its concept of humans: Does it consider all individuals to be intrinsically of equal worth in spite of their uniqueness, and hence entitled to the same social, economic, civil, and political rights; or do individuals in the society consider themselves, and those close to themselves, of greater worth than anyone else, and hence entitled to more desirable or privileged circumstances? The former egalitarian philosophy would be reflected in institutional arrangements involving cooperative actions in pursuit of common existential interests. All individuals would be considered and treated as equally entitled subjects who could not be exploited and dominated by other individuals or groups, and whose rights to develop their individuality freely and fully would be assured and respected, subject to the same rights of all others. The latter, nonegalitarian philosophy, on the other hand, is reflected in institutional structures which encourage competitive behavior in pursuit of narrowly perceived, egotistical interests. All individuals and groups strive to get ahead of others, consider themselves entitled to privileged conditions and positions, and view and treat others as potential means to be used, exploited, and dominated in pursuit of egotistical goals.

It should be noted here that the value dimension of equality-inequality is not a continuous one, for while there are degrees of inequality which may be increased or decreased, there are no degrees of equality. A distribution or allocation is either equal or unequal, and humans may be deemed equal or unequal in intrinsic worth. Therefore, the notion of 'more equality' which is used frequently in political discourse by reform-minded persons is intrinsically self-contradictory. Inequality, on the other hand, is a continuous dimension and it is, therefore, appropriate to speak of increases or decreases in inequality. This distinction is important in order to avoid confusion in political thought and action, and in order not to interpret the advocacy of 'more equality' as commitment to equality. More equality merely means a different level of inequality: it is, thus, a veiled commitment to the perpetuation of the guiding principles of inequality and privilege.

Two additional value dimensions need to be considered here because of their relevance to developmental, allocative, and distributional processes: Cooperation—competition; and collectivity-orientation—self-orientation. These two dimensions are related to, and interact with each other. They are also related to, and interact with the value dimension earlier discussed, equality-inequality. However, the relations among these three dimensions are not fixed. They vary in different societies and at different times in the same society.

The dimensions are continuous variables, which means that societies may be located at extreme or intermediate positions with references to these dimensions. The dominant value orientations of specific societies usually involve unique combinations of cooperation and competition, and of collectivity-orientation and self-orientation in the context of equality or different levels of inequality. Different societies may thus be visualized as located at different positions in a three-dimensional value space.

Collectivity-orientation, it should be noted, is not a negation of individuality and self-actualization. It is, however, a negation of 'rugged individualism,' which is a value orientation that disregards the rights of others to self-actualization. Collectivity-orientation may in fact be a necessary, though not sufficient, condition for the full and free development of everyone's individuality.[3]

SOCIAL DEVELOPMENT

Based on the conceptions of social policies and of social-policy-relevant value dimensions presented here, social development may be thought of as a specific configuration of social policies, chosen consciously by a population in accordance with egalitarian, cooperative, and collectivity-oriented value premises, aimed at enhancing systematically:

> the overall quality of life or the existential milieu of the entire society;
> the circumstances of living of all individual members and segments of the society; and
> the quality of all human relations.

Understood in this way, social development involves philosophical, biological, ecological, psychological, social, economic, and political dimensions. In contradistinction to conventional, by now outdated, notions of economic growth and development, the central criterion for evaluating social development is evenly shared, balanced progress of the entire population of a region, or of the globe, towards enhanced collective, segmental, and individual well-being. Genuine social development seems, therefore, predicated upon the conscious acceptance and systematic implementation of a configuration of developmental, allocative, and distributive social policies, the interaction and combined effects of which would be conducive to the comprehensive objectives specified here.

SOCIAL POLICIES FOR SOCIAL DEVELOPMENT: GENERAL CONSIDERATIONS

First among social policy clusters essential for social development is the identification, selection, and development of an appropriate range and mix of resources, sufficient in quantity and suitable in quality, to satisfy the basic biological and the social and psychological needs of the entire population. Policies for resource selection and development should preclude greedy, exploitative relations to the habitat of a population, as well as all forms of waste and destruction of real wealth which consists of land, water, wildlife, vegetation, natural raw materials, humans and human products. Such policies would involve effective measures for conservation and recycling of the natural resource basis of life while deriving sustenance from that base. Related to these policies would also be measures aimed at achieving and maintaining a dynamic balance of natural resources, the prevailing scientific and technological capacity to produce life-sustaining and enhancing goods from these resources, and the size of the population.

Next, social development is predicated upon policies conducive to effective and efficient organization of productive processes for the transformation of natural resources by means of human creativity and labor into the goods and services required to sustain and enhance the life of the population. Policies organizing the productive processes include also policies dealing with the education and preparation of society's 'human capital,' the release and development of the available creative physical and intellectual potential of people of all ages. Policies in this domain must also deal with the conservation, maintenance, and renewal of means of production, and with the allocation and investment of human resources and capital to the various branches of production. There is also need for policies concerning the size and location of productive units, the scope of production in various branches and units, the manner in which production and production units are controlled, and production decisions are made by those working in the units and by various local, regional, and transregional groups and institutions. Finally, in this domain, policies are needed to facilitate cooperation, coordination, integration, exchange, and joint planning among the separate production units, branches of production, the aggregate productive enterprise in a region, and units, branches, and aggregate economies in other regions all over the globe.

Since, by definition, social development is concerned with enhancing qualitative aspects of human existence, as much as it is concerned with quantitative aspects of production, it is predicated also on policies resulting in a division of labor that is cooperative rather than competitive, flexible, and fair. Such a division of labor would also involve equal recognition and equal rewards for every type of work, and whenever feasible, rotation of workers among roles which differ in intrinsic rewards. Finally, such a division of labor would involve equal rights for all to participate in the productive enterprise of society, and hence would eliminate the absurdity, so prevalent in competitive, profit motivated societies, of unemployment of workers, land, and plants while human needs remain unmet, and production is out of step with these needs.

Needless to say, social development as conceived here is also predicated upon flexible, egalitarian distribution to all members and segments of society of the concrete wealth produced by their labor, upon equal access to the human services it administers, upon equal civil liberties and political rights, and upon according to all equal recognition, honor, and prestige. It follows that implicit in genuine social development are patterns of role allocation and rights distribution which conform to the notion 'to each according to need, from each according to capacity.'

Finally, social development is predicated upon avoidance of exploitation and domination of humans and natural resources in other parts of the globe. All forms of exploitation and domination beyond a given society's boundaries inevitably negate and destroy internal processes of social development since foreign exploitation and domination always involve exploitative and domineering human relations within a society by powerful, ruling elites toward large segments of their own people. Internal and external exploitation and oppression complement and reinforce each other. They are manifestations of the same underlying principles and dynamics, to wit: a commitment to inequality, and hence a readiness to use other humans as means or objects in the greedy pursuit of hegemony, privilege, and profit for oneself, one's tribe, or one's nation. Genuine social development can never result from such attitudes and actions, only imbalanced pseudo development—illusions or caricatures of true social development. The alienating and oppressive internal milieu of societies who were, or are, practicing colonial or neo-colonial exploitation and oppression, reflects these contradictions. It demonstrates the incompatibility between social development, understood as egalitarian enhancement of the quality of life for all, and the practice of exploitation at home and abroad in pursuit of maldistributed, imbalanced economic growth.

It should be noted here, that while foreign exploitation and domination in any form are incompatible with genuine social development, foreign trade among societies living in different parts of the globe is not, as long as such trade involves voluntary exchanges of different types of resources on the basis of equality among trading partners. Such exchanges as well as all forms of mutual aid among neighboring and distant peoples are apt to promote the social development of all participants.

SOCIAL POLICY STRATEGIES TOWARDS SOCIAL DEVELOPMENT

Considering the conception of social policies and social development articulated so far in this essay, what specific social policies can be expected to set in motion, and maintain the momentum, of processes of social development? When social development means evenly shared, balanced progress of entire populations towards enhancement of the circumstances of living, the quality of life, and the quality of all human relations, it is predicated upon social policies shaped by a humanistic, egalitarian, and democratic philosophy. For evenly shared progress can materialize only when social policies are designed consciously to treat every human as a subject, of intrinsically equal worth, entitled to equal social, economic, civil, and political rights, liberties, responsibilities, and recognition. Hence, whenever institutional structures and dynamics of a society are in conflict with such a philosophy, initiating and maintaining the momentum of social development requires fundamental transformations of the institutional order and of the value premises that sustain and reinforce that order.

Productive Resources as a Public Trust

What then, is the meaning, in terms of specific social policies, of such fundamental transformations of the institutional order that would be conducive to genuine social development? It means, above all else, that the productive resources of a society, its land, water, and other natural resources, its machinery and factories, as well as its accumulated stock of scientific knowledge and technology must not be owned or controlled by individuals or by small segments of the population, and must not be used to secure privileged circumstances of living for propertied classes or other powerful groups such as bureaucratic elites, intellectual elites, etc. These sources of all wealth must be transformed into, and maintained in perpetuity as, a collectively owned and democratically controlled public trust or 'common-wealth,' appropriate shares of which would be allocated for use, not for ownership, to people working and living by themselves or in groups. The public trust of productive resources would be administered and preserved in a manner that would assure every one's participation throughout life as equally entitled decision maker, producer, and consumer, using everyone's capacities, and satisfying everyone's needs for goods and services. Privately owned property would be limited for goods destined for personal use, such as clothing, homes, household appliances, etc., and for personal consumption, such as food.

Allocation of Productive Resources

Next, social policies, conducive to social development, should establish priority rules concerning the allocation of productive resources, to assure that goods and services which meet the basic needs of the entire population for food, homes, clothing, health, education, communication, etc., are produced in appropriate quantities and quality before less essential goods and services are produced. Policies should also promote balance among population size and needs, ecological considerations, and the reality of ultimate limits of natural resources, by prudently adjusting birth rates, and by precluding all avoidable waste and destruction of natural resources and human capacities. Such waste and destruction may be inevitable when processes of production are shaped by dynamics intrinsic to the drive for profit and the accumulation of privately controlled wealth. If production were geared systematically to meeting the needs of a population through a stable and balanced supply of high quality, long lasting goods and services, producers would no longer need to engage in economically irrational practices, induced now by the competitive scramble for market shares and profits, such as artificially inflated and manipulated levels and patterns of consumption, model changes involving, not improvements, but marginal variations, transitional and arbitrary fashions, built-in obsolescence, deceptive advertising and image-building aimed at generating artificial and often harmful needs and status symbols, etc.

Harmonizing Agricultural and Industrial Production

Another policy strategy essential to social development is the promotion of balanced integration of agricultural and industrial production. A steady and reliable supply of nutritious food is obviously a *sine qua non* of social development. Accordingly, policies that sacrifice the production and supply of food and the quality of village life by shifting humans and natural resources from rural-agricultural toward urban-industrial development which primarily benefits the perceived interests of established, powerful, wealth-holding elites, are clearly counterindicated. Such policies usually result in mass migration from potentially healthy rural environments into urban slums, traditional breeding grounds for human misery, exploitation, and manifold human and social pathology. While conventional economists tend to argue that the benefits of concentrated and accelerated industrialization, in accordance with capitalist principles, would in time trickle down to all segments of a population, history, since the industrial revolution in Europe and North America, as well as over recent decades in Asia, Africa, and South America, suggests that this theory has never really worked, and that whatever benefits result from such industrialization, tend to flow away from working people who produce them and who bear a heavy cost, upward, towards privileged and frequently unproductive segments of societies.

Industry: Servant or Master?

To assure compatibility between industrial and social development, industry must never be considered an end in itself, nor a means toward the generation and accumulation of privately controlled wealth. Instead, industry would have to be designed as a powerful instrument to serve the well-being of the entire population, rather than people being used as tools to serve the well-being of profit oriented industry. Accordingly, social development oriented policies should facilitate geographic dispersion of industry throughout a country to where people live, and to where raw materials and sources of natural energy are easily available. Furthermore, policies should steer industrial production primarily toward the high priority needs of the population—food, homes, clothing, health, education, communication, etc.—and away from wasteful production of non-essentials. Locating industry in villages, small towns, and regional centers, and relating it to the needs of such communities, rather than exclusively locating it in, and relating it to, major metropolitan centers and their distorted needs; transforming the function of industry from serving the interests of privileged groups to serving the interests of all people; and finally, transferring responsibilities for directing industry from private, absentee owners and their representatives to workers, consumers, local communities, and the democratic institutions of society, can be expected to facilitate the harmonious integration of industrial enterprises into the agricultural base of the population, into both rural and urban life, and thus into processes of genuine social development.

Related to industrialization is also the question whether productive enterprises should be organized along labor-intensive or capital-intensive principles. This policy choice would have to depend in any particular instance on the relative availability of human and other resources at given stages of social and technological development. As with all other policy issues, the decision criterion should be the common interests of society, broadly conceived, rather than narrowly defined criteria of profitability. Hence, the optimal solution, to be promoted through appropriate social policies, should involve full employment of all available human resources in constructive, meaningful, and intrinsically rewarding productive activities, supported by tools, machinery, science, and technology to enhance effectiveness and efficiency, to eliminate unhealthy and damaging aspects of production, and to reduce hard and unpleasant labor as far as is compatible with prudent conservation of the environment and its natural resources.

Restructuring Work: Employing Human Resources to Meet Human Needs
Some further observations seem indicated here concerning policies which would shape the organization and the quality of

work and the division of labor in a manner conducive to social development. The most fundamental principle in this context ought to be that everyone is entitled, and has a responsibility, to participate in the aggregate labor of society. This means that whatever the total amount of labor which society requires to sustain and enhance its way of life, be that amount large or small, it is to be shared evenly among all members of society. Human employment and the wasteand alienation resulting from it would thus be abolished.

Another important principle in this context is that all occupations within a rationally designed system of production and services ought to entitle individuals engaging in them to roughly equal rewards in terms of claims against society's aggregate product, as well as in terms of social recognition or prestige. Such equal shares of returns to all workers would reflect the premise that all work is necessary in generating the aggregate social product, that it consequently represents a necessary service to society, that it ought to be considered of equal intrinsic worth to society's well-being and should entitle workers to equal circumstances of living.

While, then, all work roles of a rationally designed system of production and services would be deemed equally important, and hence equal in worth, the experience of individuals engaging in different occupations would, nevertheless, vary widely in quality. Moreover, different individuals are also likely to develop preferences and talents for different types of work. All this means is that different levels of intrinsic satisfaction would result from different occupations for individuals of like capacities and inclinations, and that differences in talents and taste among individuals would be additional sources of variation in experience. Since work roles ought to be allocated in a manner providing roughly equal returns and satisfaction, these differences inherent in occupations and people ought to be considered and compensated for through social policies that structure the division of labor in society, including the choices of, the preparation for, and the access to different work roles.

These considerations of work in relation to social development reveal a multiplicity of potentially conflicting objectives which need to be reconciled through appropriate social policies. Before suggesting such policies, the objectives will be briefly restated:

— all tasks a society considers necessary to sustain and enhance its way of life must be carried out by, and hence allocated to, some individuals;

— all occupations necessary to sustain and enhance a society's way of life are to be deemed of equal intrinsic worth, and should entitle individuals engaging in them to equal claims against the aggregate social product, and to equal social recognition;

— work ought to be directed by the workers themselves, and ought to be meaningful, constructive and a medium for self-actualization, while serving also the interests of the community; individuals should be free, as far as possible, to choose occupational roles in accordance with their capacities, talents, tastes, and interests.

Policies to Organize Work and Distribute Rights

Appropriate combinations of the following policy measures should overcome the conflicts and contradictions implicit in these objectives. First, production should be directed by the workers performing it, and the production processes should not be split into minute, repetitive, and meaningless units, so as not to destroy opportunities for expressing individual craftsmanship and creativity, and for deriving a sense of pride and accomplishment while producing goods or services of high quality and aesthetic value. Second, unhealthy, dangerous, heavy, unpleasant, and routine work should be performed by machines before other, more desirable work is mechanized. Third, work considered less desirable, or undesirable, which cannot be mechanized for various reasons, ought to be shared equally by all. This could be accomplished by allocating specified stages of the life cycle to the performance of such less desirable tasks, or by taking turns in undertaking these tasks throughout life. Fourth, opportunities ought to be provided to change one's occupation at various stages of life, to engage in different occupations at the same time, or to rotate among different roles over time. Special efforts ought to be made to overcome the prevailing, nearly absolute separation between physical and mental work, and the differential social valuation of these work domains. Next, access to preparatory channels for all occupations ought to be completely open to all, and all vestiges of role allocation by way of caste or class channels or by sex must be eliminated.

Finally, the distribution of rights, or of claims to shares of society's aggregate wealth and product ought to be completely separated from the division of labor. Rights and claims ought to be distributed as universal, equal entitlements rather than as task-specific, differential rewards. Everyone ought to be entitled to a roughly equal share to satisfy all socially sanctioned needs throughout life by virtue of being a contributing member of one's community and society, irrespective of the type of work one engages in.

Conducting Public Affairs

Another essential component of a strategy for social development, the last to be discussed here although its role is crucial, is policies that shape the conduct of public affairs, the patterns of governance, leadership, and decision making. As conceived in this essay, social development implies that choices and decisions affecting the circumstances of living of people be arrived at in a thoroughly democratic fashion, with everyone who may be affected by a decision being informed about all relevant aspects, and having an 'equal voice,' that is equal rights, opportunities, and power in determining the outcome. Representative democracy, when practiced in an essentially inegalitarian context of interest group competition, inevitably falls short of these criteria. Hence it needs to be transcended, and replaced by political institutions conducive to participatory democracy. The basic units of such political institutions would not be isolated individuals, but self-governing community groups, small enough to permit close personal relations, yet large enough to assure economic viability and social continuity. They could be producer-consumer collectives or merely neighborhood groups. They would share social, economic, cultural, child-rearing, educational and recreational functions and concerns. These groups would vary in size and in internal patterns and life styles. They would be linked in local and translocal networks or federations which in turn might form more encompassing, democratic macrostructures. Coordination and integration among these many entities would be achieved through local, regional, and transregional representative assemblies. These assemblies would have to be designed in a manner that would assure full and informed participation of all units and levels in decisions shaping their existence. Issues for deliberation and decision could originate at any level, but would always have to be examined on all levels so that local and trans-local perspectives would be taken into consideration and reconciled before decisions are reached.

Such a multi-level, political system of decentralized, yet coordinated and integrated, self-governing groups could not function effectively, unless every unit accepted egalitarian and collectivity-oriented value premises as primary decision criteria for all issues, and refrained from competitive interactions derived from a scarcity mentality and a zero-sum model. Commitment to egalitarian values, and the emergence of non-competitive attitudes would lead to cooperative approaches in sharing and allocating productive resources, and in producing and distributing goods and services, setting thus in motion a process of plus-sum dynamics towards a reality and mentality of evenly shared adequacy and well-being.

Egalitarian-democratic institutions will not endure without widespread political awareness and conscientious involvement in public affairs, facilitated by an unobstructed flow of relevant information. Such political institutions could, therefore, not sanction claims for secrecy and confidential, privileged communications concerning public issues. For if people are to be free and their own masters, and if they are to share equally the responsibilities and entitlements of citizenship, then individuals assigned to public service roles for a specified time, must under no circumstances be permitted to withhold information from the sovereign people. It should be realized in this context that behind all claims for secrecy and privileged communications lurks usually an evil purpose involving either the defense of existing, unfair and unjust conditions or the intent to create, and benefit from, such conditions. Just and fair objectives and purposes, on the other hand, can always be discussed and confronted openly among equals.

Leadership in an egalitarian-democratic commonwealth means service to people, not control and rule over people. It involves performance of a set of tasks deemed necessary by society to maintain and enhance its way of life. The social value of these tasks is equal to that of all other tasks deemed necessary by society. Hence individuals assigned for a time to the performance of leadership functions should not be entitled to privileged circumstances of living, but should share the same life style and the same rights to goods and services as all other members of society. If leadership roles are defined as service functions not entitling individuals performing them to special rewards in the form of additional goods, services, and prestige, people will be less eager to assume these roles and to hold on to them. It may in fact become difficult to recruit volunteers for leadership roles, as their performance would require commitment of much extra time and effort. Hence these roles may eventually have to be filled by assigning everyone to take a turn.

It remains to be noted that qualifications for leadership roles are not as extraordinary and as rare as people in inegalitarian, competitive societies assume, and as leaders and their promoters pretend. In such societies, leaders invariably come from or are selected by and represent the interests of wealthy and powerful population segments. Furthermore, leadership roles in such societies entitle those who perform them to considerable privileges. Finally, these roles are also a source of patronage and corruption. Once secrecy and confidential, privileged communications are abolished, and with them the monopoly on information about public affairs, which political and economic elites now maintain, individuals who keep informed on public affairs, and will participate in their community groups in the study and disposition of public issues, will soon develop the skills necessary for dealing with such issues, for representing their groups, and for assuming leadership positions. As with many other tasks that are monopolized in the prevailing social order by various powerful groups, the real issue concerning leadership roles seems to be access and opportunity rather than unique qualifications and abilities. It should also be emphasized that in an egalitarian-democratic system the nature of leadership roles will be different, and less complex than in the context of centralized, manipulative executive power. The political institutions of egalitarian, participatory democracy will be designed in a manner that will preserve the right and responsibility of the people to make all decisions on policy in their community groups, and in their representative assemblies on local and trans-local levels. Accordingly, the primary responsibility of leaders will be the faithful execution of the people's decisions. They will be administrators, not powerful rulers.

SUMMARY

The specific policies which have been presented here as necessary components of a strategy toward social development are not isolated fragments. They are not independent, but complement one another. Their combined impact should bring about the fundamental transformations of social values, structures, and dynamics implicit in the notion of social development. What unifies these policies is the underlying humanistic, egalitarian, democratic philosophy, according to which all humans are intrinsically of equal worth, are entitled to equal rights in every sphere of life, and may not be exploited or dominated by other humans. The policies were developed by consistently applying these values and principles to the major domains of human existence and social organization, namely, the control and allocation of all productive resources, the design of productive processes and criteria for production priorities, the division of labor and the organization and valuation of work, the distribution of rights and claims to shares of the aggregate social product, and finally, the design of political institutions.

There are, of course, concepts of social development which differ fundamentally in underlying assumptions and values from a humanistic, egalitarian, and democratic conception. Adherents of such alternative positions will often acknowledge humanistic, egalitarian, and democratic values as ultimate goals, but will not use these values as guiding principles and evaluative criteria when formulating policies in the present. This avoidance tends to be rationalized as being 'realistic and practical,' while insisting on social justice here and now is being labeled as 'utopian, naive, and impractical.' Such realistic and practical approaches to social development mean that, while humans would be treated as equals some time in the future, socially structured and defined inequalities are to be accepted as a given aspect of present reality. They must not be questioned or challenged on a fundamental level, but must be reckoned with, adjusted to, and incorporated into policy formulation for social development. The result of such pragmatic development policies is at best an illusion of social development, pursued for the benefit of relatively small, yet economically and politically powerful elite groups, through exploitation and domination of economically and politically powerless majorities of the population.

History suggests that such 'pragmatic' compromise approaches to social development which acquiesce in established inequalities and injustices do not work, however well intentioned their advocates may be. They do not work for exploited majorities whose basic needs remain unsatisfied and who continue to be oppressed and alienated. Nor do these approaches work in terms of the real, long-range, human interest of the power and wealth controlling minorities. The reason for the failure of these development policies is the intensification of intra-societal conflict which usually accompanies their implementation, and which may be inevitable in view of the economic, social, and psychological dynamics generated in an inegalitarian, competitive context, and its scarcity, zero-sum mentality. The human and economic costs of maintaining an established, inegalitarian social order tend to increase exponentially in spite of sporadic patchwork efforts to save that order from collapsing. Sooner or later this process tends to reach levels of massive breakdown. To refer to this self-defeating process as social development is, of course, absurd.

The conclusion of these considerations seems inescapable. Social development, like human freedom and dignity, is indivisible. It simply cannot be secured for segments of a population at the price of exploiting and oppressing other segments. It can be achieved only for all together, or for none at all. Either all are free and equal, brothers and sisters in a universal process towards social development, or none will gain freedom and fulfilment.

J. F. X. PAIVA

6 Program Planning

Program planning in social development is still in a rudimentary stage. Very few social programs have been systematically planned and monitored under specified guidelines. Even fewer have been properly documented or have had their outcomes evaluated.

In social development the task of program planning is translating social policies and strategies into concrete services and specific activities. Social development as elaborated here aims at improving the quality of individual life and raising the level of living for all through planned and responsive social and institutional changes. The process involves integration of social and economic objectives, structural as well as institutional changes, and feedback in the process of balanced development.[1]

Program planning in this context is defined by key prerequisites, strategies, and planning functions. The prerequisites for program planning are planning machinery, national policies for social development, need perception and participation, resource availability, and decision making. The strategic approaches in program planning are discussed under four models. These models are applied to different target systems. Finally, certain dimensions of choice are analyzed to define specific planning functions and activities. These choices are related to resource allocations, the nature and content of social provisions, funding procedures, and the structuring and delivery of the program. Evaluation and feedback raise issues of continuing importance for the process of program planning.

I. Some Prerequisites for Program Planning and Development

1. ADMINISTRATIVE STRUCTURE AND AUSPICES

Program planning and development require the existence of an administrative structure. The thrust and pace of development may vary according to the location of the program planning structures. For example, the initiation of a social development program and the process of organizing its network of components may differ if the program is located in a primarily economic context, in a health and welfare context, or in a planning agency without specific affiliation to substantive program areas.

The planning structure will also vary according to the nature of the population group and the political entity for whom the program is being considered. Thus what kind of planning unit is being developed under one or another auspices for a particular target group at a specific political level makes a good deal of difference. Wherever the planning structure may be and at whatever political level, the special demands of social development call for a close interrelationship among the different programs, target population, political units, and levels of administration.

2. NATIONAL POLICIES

It is rather difficult to conceive of program planning outside the context of a national or societal policy. Values and preferences are an integral part of social programs. In the pursuit of individual needs or the well-being of a social group, a central direction toward what is preferable for a given societal system as a whole needs to be explained. With respect to such pervading questions as social justice, human freedom, and the equitable distribution of goods and opportunities, limited choices cannot be bargained for in the market place. Only within a national, sometimes even an international, perspective can choices be made for promoting individual and societal development. Program planning in its designing phases might be able to develop a set of linkages in which such national directions and support are crucial even when planning at comparatively small community levels.

3. PARTICIPATION

Program planning evolves out of a joint exploration between

people and the agents of change. When a partnership prevails in the task of development, chances are better that social development goals will be satisfactorily achieved.

As consumers of social services or recipients of the impacts of change measures, the people represent a source of expertise. The change agents on the other hand possess an expertise based on their employment experience or their professions. Change strategies will be more effective when there is greater congruency between the people and the change agents brought about by process of mutual education and persuasion.

4. RESOURCE AVAILABILITY

Availability of resources obviously affects the scope, content, and pace of social development processes. Energy for program development cannot begin to grow without energy to initiate the process. Sometimes programing for social development will yield new resources. In most cases lack of resource availability presents a difficulty at the beginning. Policy decisions for social development may also indicate resources for implementation. Where this is not so, analysis of resources becomes part of the program development process.

5. DECISION MAKING

Program planning assumes that some decisions have already been made at other levels about the kind of structure and the mode of service delivery. While the final decision may come from a lawfully constituted authority, planning must reflect the problems, values, or needs in the different segments of the total social system. Once a final governmental decision has been made, a process of interpretation or evaluation may follow leading to clarification of the decision and the necessary plan modification for effective implementation. Decision making, therefore, involves participation at different levels and a continuous process in the machinery for social development.

II. ALTERNATIVE APPROACHES TO PROGRAM PLANNING

The strategies and approaches to program planning are likely to be affected by factors such as perception of needs, characteristics of social institutions (macro and micro), recognition and utilization of change processes, nature of partnership in development, and availability of resources. Eugen Pusic has used two key concepts to analyze these factors in social and economic development: energy and structure.[2] Energy is interpreted to mean resources such as employment, health, and income maintenance services. Structure is defined as institution building and social structuring of the change process. The two factors interact and contribute to each other. The degree of energy and structure present in a social system constitutes the level of social and economic development.

The task of program planning in this framework is to examine through assessment and a continuous process of institutional evaluation (1) what kind of energy and structure a system needs and to what extent or degree; and (2) the nature of the interaction between energy and structure that will keep changing the status of what is needed for the first task.

In order to facilitate this process of program planning, social systems may be regarded as having a high or low degree of energy and structure. Thus there are four basic types of social systems from the perspective of planning for social development.

1. *High Energy and High Structure*

This type of social system has optimum potentials for program development. For example, in new settlements where work-place and folk-place objectives are combined to develop a new way of life, the chances of successfully integrating the available resources with available structures to produce optimum results are great. This social system is more responsive than other situations in meeting human needs and fashioning a quality of relationship in keeping with the concepts of social justice and equity.

Examples of such development are the polders of the Netherlands, the new satellite towns around Greater London, and the resettlement of people along river basins in some of the developing countries. Even with optimum potential, high energy and high structure, these settlements have not necessarily achieved the maximum potentials of development. These social systems still may require the needed interaction for shaping and furthering social development.

2. *High Energy and Low Structure*

The health, education, and welfare systems of the United States are an example of this category. There are adequate resources in the system for generating social development. But correspondingly, the institutions have not yet accepted health and welfare as universal human rights. Program planning for social development will be aimed here at that kind of institution building, social structure change, and the reallocation of resources for raising the quality of human life for all but especially for those most deprived, and for safeguarding human values with the growth of social and industrial technology.

3. *Low Energy and High Structure*

The social welfare system as operative in the U.S.S.R. is an example of this category. The paucity of resources is not able to generate the needed interaction with the well established structure for the realization of social development goals.

The question arises whether a lessening of investments in structure may not yield more resources for energy. The appropriateness of such a strategy could only be answered by an in-depth assessment within the framework of the parameters of the development task.

4. *Low Energy and Low Structure*

In this category are those areas of developing countries with a predominance of poverty and few structures to cope with the problems. Endemic poverty in the regions of the developed world such as in urban ghettoes or in isolated rural areas are also characterised by little energy and little structure.

The critical question in all these types is what kind and quantity or what proportion of energy and structure inputs are needed to foster development. Once a decision has been made, the next strategy of program planning is to manage the processing of inputs that will influence the interaction between energy and structure. These are processes of intersystemic integration.

INTERSYSTEMIC INTEGRATION

1. *Comprehensiveness*

Essentially, this consists in bringing together whatever is considered relevant to the development task. Political, administrative, economic, social, cultural, and other variables are looked at for their relevance in contributing to development. At the same time the economy of efforts demands identifying those considered crucial to the development outcome.

2. *Integration*

Here the concern is that the crucially important variables are not merely strung together but made to fit. For example, in designing a housing project, transportation, employment, and the tenants committee must be identified as a system of dovetailing parts in planning a role for the tenants committee and establishing linkages between transportation, access to employment, and other services.

3. *Balance*

Here a decision must determine the nature of a proportionate balance between systems or parts of systems needed for desirable outcomes. The degree and kind of employment programs, kinds of institution building tasks, and the optimum relation between these tasks will determine a proportionate balance in the provision of programs and setting up of the institutional process. The proportion in the 'systemic mixture' (selected elements in a manpower system, for example) and 'intersystemic mixture' (manpower, health, institutional linkages, for example) would largely depend on other factors present in the system which accelerate or slow down the processes of harmonious development. The same proportions in different systems could yield entirely different results. Continuous assessment and evaluation is a key factor in determining the proportion of systemic and intersystemic integration.

4. *Interdependence*

This refers to a partnership among the actors in the systems working together when viewed collectively and separately. Interdependence connotes a harmonious complementarity of roles in which each partner contributes something to the achievement of the whole. The professions, the disciplines, the sectors of development, and the citizens all have their parts to play as equal partners in the task of development. Resources, expertise, authority, and power need to be diversified and differentially considered so that there could be maximum participation and sharing in the task of development.

5. *Program Outcomes*

Program planning should lead to outcomes generally defined as desired goals of social development. These outcomes are such things as better distribution of power to enable people to participate in decision making, social mobility and access to opportunities, a broad based participation in the production and consumption of goods and services, and increase in quality of life. Program planning may also produce unintended consequences that might require modification of the group strategies or adoption of another program to deal with the side effects. Sound program planning should anticipate any side effects in the implementation process and provide measures for early detection and control.

PARADIGM: PROGRAM PLANNING PROCESS

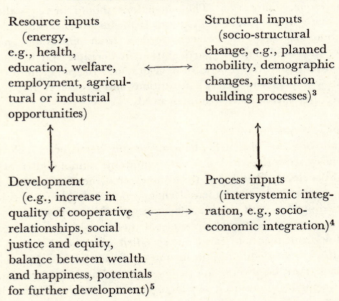

Resource inputs
(energy,
e.g., health,
education, welfare,
employment, agricultural or industrial
opportunities)

Structural inputs
(socio-structural
change, e.g., planned
mobility, demographic
changes, institution
building processes)[3]

Development
(e.g., increase in
quality of cooperative
relationships, social
justice and equity,
balance between wealth
and happiness, potentials
for further development)[5]

Process inputs
(intersystemic integration, e.g., socioeconomic integration)[4]

III. ELEMENTS OF PROGRAM PLANNING

Gilbert and Specht have provided a conceptual framework for analyzing social welfare policies.[6] This framework could be used to study the content of program planning with a view to identifying alternative approaches. Such alternatives may be based on values or on assumptions intended to explain conditions in the situation. The first three alternatives are relevant to the planning process while the fourth is primarily relevant to implementation.

1. *Bases of Social Allocations*

The key question here is who is to be the recipient of the program's allocations whether they represent goods or services or other change processes and structural arrangements. However, another important question that must accompany this is how the process of directing the program at a specific population group will contribute to major change. In other words, the fundamental nature of the objectives need to be defined and the cost benefits need to be estimated in terms of basic change.[7]

Program planning must address itself to critical issues in the area of resource allocation. The allocations should increase the level of living of the target population. It means a more equitable distribution of goods and services, freedom from oppression and injustice, increased popular participation in decision and action, and a continuity in the process of development. In short, the programs may change the society's institutions and structures and result in greater satisfaction of human needs.

2. *Nature of Social Provisions*

Alternative forms of benefits have to be considered here. Token provisions or those that deal only with symptoms cannot contribute to social development unless it were shown that they are part of a strategy to move into fundamental change policies within a specified period of time with specific allocations for this purpose.

For any given social development goal there might be a variety of possible instruments to carry out specified objectives.[8] For example, to correct inequalities in income and educational opportunities there may be several approaches: providing transportation to school system, to ensure a satisfactory level of instruction in all the schools in the areas, adequate wage supplementation to meet school costs, and diverse ways of utilizing school resources, and locating schools for all income groups within access of quality resources needed for the school; providing linkages between school programs and future employment; diversifying educational programs for a variety of occupations; ensuring linkages between industrial or economic development and education so that education is not hampered by local politics. All these instruments will vary in complexity depending on the target population, its milieu, and its connection with other social systems.

The choice of these instruments and the way they are to be selected and interconnected will depend on such important factors as priority objectives, availability of resources, the community's values, the degree of community participation, and the cost of these operations.

3. *Sources and Conditions of Funding*

The amount of funding sources and the conditions of their utilization present a variety of options to program planning. It is possible that certain funding sources may be more attuned to social development than others—whether the sources be a private financing agency or a government department. Because each of these may carry stipulations regarding the manner of appropriations and the conditions under which they are to be spent, there may be few alternatives when it comes to funding. But motivations other than social development may be the purpose of some granting bodies. This in itself may not be bad as long as it is possible to gain acceptance and commitment for social development in the process of program planning.

The use of the funds for specific program purposes to achieve preferred goals presents several options for program planners. Here again, values, strategies, social theory, and the involvement of the target population play crucial roles in helping the planner make choices.

4. *Program Organization and Delivery*

This may be regarded as the plan implementation process during which consideration is given to alternatives with respect to the organization and structure of the program and the means to achieve development priorities through selected program activities.

Plan implementation concerns the methodology and techniques of implementing the plan to promote social development. The implementation could be carried out through timing and phasing, systems linkage, the development of infrastructures, and community participation and partnership for development. These are a few of the important instruments for implementing the program.

(a) *Timing and Phasing.* One of the characteristics of social development is that it tries to seek accelerated change within a foreseeable period of time. Normal social change processes might contribute incrementally to development through indefinite periods of time. Whereas the modernization period of the European countries took two centuries or more, the African and Asian countries have achieved this stage at least in some sectors of the society, within decades. The discrepancy between economic activities and human fulfillment is even greater in these circumstances of rapid change. Social development emphasizes human goals that need to be given paramount consideration for current realization in the race for material production. Timing and phasing is of great importance both as a strategy, as well as a development goal in itself. Assessments have to be made about how long certain programs could be maintained at a service level until development processes warrant reduction in the service inputs. The fulfillment of some program goals and activities needs to be measured in time dimensions as well as in phases of identifiable levels of certain tasks being accomplished. For instance in promoting rural development there could be several task goals: the education of young people with a focus on controlled migration to the cities; the location of agriculture related industries within distances of time and space away from large urban centers; the education of existing small farmers in cooperative enterprises, etc. The strategy of phasing makes it crucial to dovetail task goals and processes of achieving them so that one level of achievement reinforces or stimulates another. The education of young people in migration, for example, should be phased in such a manner that in a set period of time local industries are ready to absorb young people who decide not to migrate into urban areas after graduating from high school. If it works well, this might very well be the phasing out of migration and the phasing in of stages in the growth of new rural towns so that each phase has a compatible socioeconomic framework within which to grow, and to establish both vertical and horizontal ties that facilitate setting the stage for the next growth phase.

(b) *Systems Linkages.* To achieve socioeconomic integration and change in institutions and social structures, different types of linkages have to be made with relevant systems and their representatives.[9] For example, in the effort to raise income levels, functional linkages may consist of dovetailing income maintenance services with education and family counselling; coordinating employment training services or provision of employment opportunities with planning for economic development; involving community members with income maintenance effort to motivate acceptance of a phased support for dependency programs before moving on to productive effort to enhance community life; and sharing information about the program through diffusive linkages at various points in the system's communication channels. Similar linkage concepts are to be utilized in institution development and in social structure changes.

(c) *Infrastructures.* While planning may take place to effect socio-economic integration and to forge linkages between the actors or systemic processes, there might yet remain the problem of not having mechanisms or structures to facilitate the linkages so essential for promoting development. Infrastructures are needed to connect systems to make the exchanges among them viable and continuous.

For example, to cite an illustration from the developing world, in trying to free the village producer from the oppression of inordinate money lending and repayment, new and convenient money lending facilities are offered. But when the villager is ready to sell his produce at a critical time related to his own needs and the agricultural cycle, if he cannot find convenient markets, he is soon involved in debt again by selling his produce to the nearest buyer. Obviously then, mobile units to buy produce on the spot and then store it safely until selling time are an important and needed infrastructure. Institutional changes become a serious challenge for introducing such infrastructures. Thus economic and social enmeshing are needed in intricate ways that could only be done through careful assessment and planning of various steps to achieve the program goals after considering different alternatives.

(d) *Participation and Partnership for Development.* This is a major mechanism for involving people in program planning and development and for motivating them towards their own betterment. The same could be said of those in other systems besides that of the recipient of goods and services for promoting development. Participation is not only for creating a psychological feeling of commitment and involvement, which is not to be minimized, but also for creating a source of new knowledge for better decisions. Partnership for development is an identification of all those systems and their leadership whose concerted action and coordinated tasks are necessary for the phased accomplishment of objectives.

Social development by its very nature involves the bringing together of relevant organizations and institutions. Family planning, for example, cannot be done effectively without dovetailing the effort of economic planners and representatives of industry, public health workers, social work departments, teachers in the school system, religious leaders, groups with special interest in either increasing or reducing birth rates, demographers, housing authorities, food and nutrition specialists, etc. The total family planning system in itself needs to be related to other program activities projected for social development such as education, employment, and income maintenance. In some cases functions or interests overlap or they need to be coordinated either as complementary efforts or supplementary programs to support each other's efforts.

A whole network of cooperative effort of varying dimensions and intensity seems necessary to promote the social process involved in program development. The feasible answer to this complex situation would be to define periods of activity more relevant than others at certain phases of the operation, and secondly, more intense interrelationships with a few periods of activity identified as crucial to the successful operation of certain phases of the program.

Social development is essentially a partnership operation— systems, resources, people, disciplines, professionals, etc. In program planning, therefore, provisions have to be made for qualitative and quantitative involvement of the actors. Obviously to involve everyone is neither functional nor feasible. Different phases of the program may need different realignments of participants in the political process. A constant challenge is to simplify these processes, to make them sufficiently meaningful for improving the quality of decision making, and to maximize the content of the programs for a series of progressive changes. The techniques of this aspect of program planning and development involve more than community participation which is extensively covered in the literature on community development.

These are only a few of the tasks to be undertaken in implementing the operation. The total situation in the social development context may suggest other elements from which the program strategies will have to be chosen.

IV. EVALUATION AND RESEARCH

It is both appropriate and important to close with a consideration of evaluation, for program evaluation is one of the processes essential to development. There are some important issues relating to evaluation which need to be discussed for the planning and implementation of social programs.

Social development tasks present innumerable problems for research. In the first place the processes of social development are not complete without a machinery for adequate evaluation. Provision for both long-term and short-term research as an integral part of program planning and development must exist. It is important to know which combinations of social and economic variables yield better results for institutional change and which choices among alternatives contribute more to raising levels of living. A few more areas relevant for social development research follow.

1. *Strategies for Utilizing Change Forces*

While there is much in the literature about intervention, there are fewer studies about harnessing the already active forces of change. These change forces have not been adequately studied in order to formulate strategies for program planning. Program objectives can be more realistically reached if the plans could be tied to forces already proceeding favorably. For example, in a small town where federal housing brings increases of economic activity, community integration between majority and minority groups could be better achieved through task objectives in the development of the community economy. Such an objective (community cohesion) has to be consciously planned for in utilizing the unifying forces of a new industry or minimizing with equal deliberateness such undesirable concomitants as resentment towards newcomers which new industries bring into communities. Working with the already existing processes of change or generating such forces or transforming them to be accountable in social development terms could be an important part of program planning. This ecological approach follows its own momentum and patterns of formation which we need to use in developing our program.

2. *Unplanned Results*

In the same context unplanned results of planned intervention need to be maximized if they are desirable and minimized if they are undesirable. Could we develop a strategy to cope with such unexpected consequences of our planning efforts? This is a very natural area for an evaluation and research component in program planning.

3. *Systems Linkage*

This involves various strategies to bring together systems and actors to facilitate and integrate the processes of social development. Such linkages represent the interrelationship of programs, professions, disciplines, and various politics in a given social system. Research efforts need to be directed to the study of variables involved in these linkages in the process of program planning and implementation.

4. *Policies and Policy Research*

We have discussed earlier the vitally important matter of a central or national policy within which social development goals could be realized. There is, however, a complex two-way process which needs to be identified. The different politics in the micro and macro systems need their own social development policies which could provide enough momentum for structuring national policies. This tension between the national and the local or individual should generate a viable structure for social development policy. Research in these processes provides insights into the problem of the adjustment between the individual and the societal system, a necessary feature of social development. It is also important to point out that national policies alone may not be adequate to provide the impetus for social development. The international arena could also be critically important in providing a policy framework for national or even local and individual social development. Program planning and development has feedbacks to policy formulation and interpretation, and these feedbacks are generated from research and evaluation.

SALIMA OMER

7 Institution Building

WHAT HISTORY SHOWS

A historical analysis of the efforts of developing countries to foster economic and political progress shows that, although these countries have had some success in the economic field, their attempts at political stability have been less fortunate. There are of course exceptions and the exceptions, precisely because they deviate from the norm of instability, provide us with models of successful institution building. The aim of this chapter is first to elaborate a conceptual framework of institution building and then to consider two illustrations of this—the Chinese communes and the kibbutzim of Israel. While the primary focus of the chapter is on developing countries, the principles enunciated and the theory of institution building have applicability to advanced nations also.

The most important task of developing countries is to achieve economic growth along with social justice. Another major task is the setting up of a political system that can ensure increase in production and economic well-being for the entire population rather than a limited few. Most developing countries that have achieved independence in the recent past—those emerging countries which have increased the number of nations represented at the UN from 51 to 151 within the period 1947–79—seem to have been until very recently preoccupied with economic growth as the panacea for all evils. At the same time their choice of a political system to achieve economic growth has in most cases been the model favored by their former colonial rulers. But the politics and economics of the emerging nations as a whole have not added up to development as a brief look at their successes and failures indicates.

I. PRODUCTIVITY

According to estimates of the Center for Development Planning, Projections, and Policies of the United Nations Secretariat, during the period 1968–73 the Gross Domestic Product of developing countries increased at an annual rate of 6·2 percent. The growth of per capita G D.P. was, however, only 3·4 percent. The per capita increase of G.D.P. for developing countries in Africa was 2·1 percent; Eastern Asia and the Pacific, 3·2 percent; Western Asia, 5·8 percent; and Latin America and the Caribbean, 3·4 percent. In contrast, the per capita G.D.P. for the developed market economies increased at an annual average rate of 3·7 percent; and centrally planned economies, 5·5 percent.[1] In the developing regions, per capita income (a fairly good indicator of general prosperity) increased at a rather slow rate compared to that of the other, more affluent, half of the world. This is not to deny the industrial progress which emerging nations have achieved over the past two or three decades. Developing countries now produce about two-thirds of all consumer goods, 40 to 50 percent of intermediate goods and 20 to 30 percent of capital goods. The production of electric energy alone multiplied by seven in Asia, five in Africa and four in Latin America in 20 years.

In spite of some figures that illustrate progress and development in certain sectors, the fact remains that 66 percent of the world population, constituting the developing world, produces only 12·5 percent of the world's goods and services, its Gross National Product. The modernizing strategies of the developing countries themselves have further aggravated internal dualism and regional disparities. During the early stages of independence, the new nations almost completely ignored the agricultural sector that provides 45 to 50 percent of the developing world's G.N.P. and employs 65 to 70 percent of its labor force. Before the mid-1960s only 15 percent of the Indian Public development expenditure was devoted to agriculture, though it contributed 46 percent of the national product and employed 70 percent of the population.[2]

II. EDUCATION

During the past decade 1960–70, the number of students worldwide enrolled in the primary, secondary and higher levels of education increased from 325 million to 482 million, an average increase of 4·1 percent. The largest increase in absolute terms was 100 million in primary education, although secondary and tertiary education experienced faster annual growth rates, 5·1 and 8·8 percent respectively. Public expenditure on education as a share of the world's G.N.P. rose from 3·5 percent in 1960 to 5·1 percent in 1970. The developed countries spent 5·4 percent of their G.N.P. and the developing countries 3·2 percent in 1970, whereas in 1960 they spent 3·7 and 2·4 percent, respectively. The ratios are an indication of the widening gap in expenditure on education between developed and developing countries. The lion's share of money spent on education (nearly $150 billion) was accounted for by the developed countries, while the developing countries spent only $12 billion.[3]

The financial outlay in education and phenomenal increase in enrollment has not altered the reality of children and young adults in developing countries being deprived of even the most rudimentary education. A statement regarding World Bank activities on behalf of education highlights the problem. 'Among 39 countries in which the World Bank has had recent lending operations in education the median primary enrollment is 70 percent; the range is 8 percent (Somalia) to 97 percent (Greece). At the secondary level for the same group of countries in the mid-sixties the median enrollment ratio is 13 percent and the range is 2 percent (Tanzania) to 70 percent (Ireland). The median percentage of total students studying for vocational subjects is 11 percent and in higher education the median enrolled in courses of engineering, medicine, science and agriculture is 21 percent.'[4] How relevant present education is to the needs of people and the world situation is an issue that goes beyond the scope of this chapter.

III. POLITICS

Most developing countries have experienced difficulties and turmoil in their political life. The transition from colonial rule to free democracies has been beset by tremendous problems. Many African, Asian and Latin American countries have failed to establish stable civilian government and in a number of instances the army has stepped in. Rostow refers to the endemic political turbulence of the developing world which yielded some 67 irregular changes in government between the years 1961 and 1968: Latin America, 16; Africa, 26; the Near East and South Asia, 11.[5] Since Rostow's study, political instability has continued to take its toll—

in Argentina, Chile, Bangladesh, and in India which was long considered the champion of democracy in Asia.

Briefly stated, the developing countries attempted to achieve progress through strategies of industrialization and education within political frameworks labelled democratic. They paid scant attention to indigenous social structures or native aspirations. Little or no notice was taken of the fact that the institutions of modern government, whether parliamentary or otherwise, have certain prerequisites, and that the functioning of political parties, like the exercise of universal franchise, is a formidable task in a milieu of illiteracy or in a feudal society lacking mechanisms for the expression of public opinion. Political and economic efforts that totally ignored the social aspects of development led to the following:

1. rapid urbanization because industrialization was concentrated in urban areas;
2. neglect of agriculture specifically, and rural development generally;
3. change in the social structure as industrialization gave rise to another moneyed class—the business community. The entrepreneurs took their place alongside the feudal landlords;
4. a strongly entrenched bureaucracy that was not only instrumental in creating national plans but also had a hand in implementing them and, in the process, gained control of the distribution of wealth;
5. the gradual erosion of the political structure as the masses became alienated from the political process while the vested interests of elitist groups held sway;
6. advances in economic growth which created greater social injustices and widened the gulf between the haves and the have-nots;
7. the existing dualism in society further aggravated by the educational, political and economic systems which the developing countries adopted.

Even the Green Revolution which was aimed at changing agriculture radically, increasing yields and bringing greater well-being to rural areas in fact aggravated the existing dualism in the social structure of developing countries and produced more inequities and regional disparities.[6]

CONCEPTUAL FRAMEWORK OF INSTITUTION BUILDING

By and large, the theorists of development as well as its implementors—the bureaucrats, landlords, business entrepreneurs, intellectuals and educationalists—have belonged to the elite. The great majority of people have either played no role in development or at best have participated marginally. The part intended for them was that of recipients, to partake of the benefits that would trickle down from the fountain of wealth. The failure of the distribution process in the developing world raises two major questions:

1. is it possible to achieve development along with social justice without the participation and involvement of the people themselves?
2. is it not the right and prerogative of people to decide what constitutes development and how to go about it. In other words, should not the people control the direction of development?

The answer to the first question on the basis of empirical evidence seems to be that in most developing countries of Asia, Africa and Latin America the efforts at development by and through a minority elite have by and large not led to social development—*development that could bring greater well-being to the general population*. In very rare cases such as Kuwait, social development has been achieved in the sense that the population at large has had a greater share of goods and services and this has been provided through the planning and programing of an elite.

The case of Kuwait raises some complicated issues. Kuwait is unique in its tiny size and enormous wealth and hence is not a good illustration of the typical developing country. Secondly, there is the philosophical issue of whether a small group of planners and implementors have a *right* to determine what is good, what is development, and what sacrifices are to be made. To take a stand on this last issue means the acceptance of certain values, and there is no reason why the statement of values should not be explicit. The assumption here is that *development along with social justice* cannot be achieved in an elitist fashion—a premise which the evidence of the past quarter of a century seems to support. From a purely ethical viewpoint, people have the right to determine what constitutes development and it is their prerogative to choose the strategies. It is only through the people's participative involvement and control that development will reflect the people's needs and aspirations and lead to a just socioeconomic order.

In order that the participative involvement can be effective, it is necessary to set up mechanisms to facilitate the process. Institution building can be the mechanism that ensures participation and control by the people. Institution building is a way to operationalize a philosophy of participation, for it means the setting up of institutions through which people enunciate policies, develop plans, implement and evaluate programs which they feel are required for their own well-being. The people themselves should define what constitutes social development, and they should measure it with yardsticks that are compatible with popular values, norms and mores.

Institutions to promote development may be set up at a variety of levels—national, regional, district, local or neighborhood— and their functions may be equally diverse—social, political, legal, police, economic. These functions may be amalgamated, i.e., co- ordinated under the roof of one agency, or they may be under the jurisdiction of many organizations. Since clustering functions or discharging them separately are both feasible, it is obviously pos- sible to allow decentralization in constructing institutions. The one requirement for the legitimacy of institutions is that they have a statutory basis. The institutions themselves may be extremely formal, complicated structures, such as a cooperative agriculture credit bank, or simple and flexible institutions like a village council or a sanitation committee. Similarly, the way business is conducted may likewise follow rigid rules or be based on friendly discussion aimed at consensus. The reason for this is the fact that the social structure of developing countries is in various stages of develop- ment, characterized by traditional methods of working and living, and by behavior patterns that determine roles for the elders in the community, for the young, and so on. If the institutions are to reflect the needs and aspirations of the people and the people are to be in charge of business, then the institutions must evolve organ- ically in accordance with popular experience and native expertise. Instead of advocating a fixed organizational structure for all insti- tutions, the architects of institutions must realize that form depends on spirit—in this instance, the culture of the masses. To build institutions supporting a just social order, the basic requirements are these:

1. that the institutions provide the people affected by programs a way to determine policy and to retain final control over outcome;
2. that the composition of organizational units not be elitist and that, as far as possible, the people themselves manage the various functions of the organization;
3. that the mechanism for achieving organizational goals be based on cooperation and consensus rather than competition;
4. that those charged with carrying out particular institutional tasks, including administrative tasks, be elected and subject to recall.

The most important prerequisite for citizen participation is that institutional development be decentralized so that citizens living within the geographic area of service may control the programs.

The achievements of a popular institution—whether economic, social or political—will depend upon the external aims of the organization (e.g., industrial productivity) and, to no small degree, organizational stamina. But in addition to the results which an organization may hope to effect in the marketplace, a popular institution can expect to achieve internal reform of equal or greater social significance. These achievements include the diffusion of power and the creation of new leadership, planning in accordance with the will of the people, greater social stability based on equality, political consciousness, and modernization capable of sustaining indigenous values.

One of the most significant results of democratic and decentralized institution building is that it involves more and more people in the process of planning and implementing activities. The diversification of activities brings about the involvement of various age groups and of people with different skills and expertise. Popular institutions, while drawing on traditional leaders, cast their nets wider to include women, the young and groups which in other circumstances are usually the recipients of services. As time goes on a new leadership emerges, diffusing power within the organization and permitting greater numbers to influence decisions at various levels.

Decentralization in institutional development gives local control to local people. Balanced regionalism allows institutions to reflect the aspirations of the people, and encourages a bottom-up approach to planning. Where orders come from the top, an organization can only react not to felt needs but to mandates, and it simply becomes an agency carrying out orders issued by state or national officials. Decentralized institutions can determine their own objectives, programs and strategies for action. They are more likely to mirror the will of the masses.

The extent of economic equality within a social structure is determined to a large extent by the choice of the economic system and the mechanisms intended to distribute wealth, income and services. It also depends on the restructuring of society, as in the case of land reform. However, even where the final steps towards equitable distribution have not been taken, grassroots institutions are still capable of combating social stratification. And the less social stratification there is, the greater will be the stability of the community. Permanent social stability is a product of just relationships. The involvement of more people in decision making, planning and implementation gives rise to social contacts hitherto unknown. In a village council, a landlord may sit side by side with a youth and be limited by the same opportunity—a single vote. The example is not meant to imply that wealth carries no weight. Of course it does, and social stratification follows on the heels of wealth. But whatever mechanisms can be used to shape society along democratic lines must be promoted. Only those who are familiar with the way in which economic and social power is wielded stand a chance of effecting change. People trained in grassroots organizing, see the need for fundamental reforms and appreciate the value of political pressure.

One of the persistent problems of developing countries has been the maintenance or introduction of stable government. Each emerging nation has sought, with greater or less sincerity, a political system that would not only support economic growth but would distribute the benefits to all citizens. As mentioned earlier, attempts to imitate American, French and British political models have failed time and time again. The setting up of political parties, the granting of universal franchise and the other trappings of Western democracy have not led inexorably to the political maturity of the masses in developing countries. A vote every three years does not change reality, especially when illiteracy and ignorance combine to make the masses susceptible to the pleas and promises of demagogues.

Political development of an enduring nature can be achieved only through the process of dealing with issues that are close to the people. Addressing community problems, people learn the meaning of democracy and internalize its values. Democracy then goes beyond the act of voting to cooperation for the collective good. It becomes a belief in human dignity implying a willingness to permit disagreement and an ability to work in harmony once a majority decision is reached. Decentralized institutions provide the opportunity for community action, teaching the doers to build their own political house.

The term modernization has been used to describe industrial growth and its effects—urbanization, prosperity, increased educational opportunity, widespread literacy and the expansion of mass communication. Most developing countries have aimed at modernization and some have attained it. But the effects have not been proper urban development, universal education or the equitable distribution of wealth. Modernization has generally resulted in economic gain for a small minority, access to higher education for some, and a little more room at the top for the new politically active elite. Industrialization in conjunction with traditional Western education has reinforced the existing dualism in developing countries. It has aggravated regional disparities and created rural-urban schisms. Because the models for industrialization have largely been Western and the introduction of technology in the developing world has more often than not been under the direction of foreigners or of personnel trained overseas, attention to indigenous values and culture has been meager.

The advantage of building community oriented institutions is that the trend towards indiscriminate modernization can be reversed and a new direction established. It is for the people to decide what aspects of modernization they wish to accept—whether they would place their main emphasis on economic development with its attendant risks or would subscribe to a different strategy of modernization which might salvage some of their traditions and protect family and community solidarity.

Worthy of discussion in this context are two examples of people's institutions—the Chinese communes and the kibbutzim of Israel.

The two are different, although each illustrates grassroots democracy. China has a centrally controlled economy but decentralizes production as well as social services through its communes, giving to people responsibility for decisions that affect their everyday lives. Israel operates within a capitalist economy. But the kibbutzim function outside the main political, economic and social mainstream of Israel and have created a sort of direct democracy in which every person has a voice in shaping the conditions and circumstances of the community.

THE CHINESE COMMUNE

China is territorially the second largest country in the world with 8·5 million square miles. It has a population of approximately 800 million.[7] Seventy-five percent of the population live in 15 percent of its territory, 80 percent of the population living in rural areas. It is not surprising then that the Chinese revolution has been largely agrarian in nature. Following earlier land reform, China took the course of transforming collective farms into communes. By 1958 the 700,000 collective farms were turned into 25,000 communes which also served as units for rural administration. This phase was marked by excessive centralization springing from a philosophy to 'collectivize and communalize' every aspect of the people's life. The inordinate control failed to spur the economy or meet the needs of the people. By 1960 the strategy and its philosophy had fallen into disrepute, and a policy of decentralization was adopted. The 25,000 communes were increased to 74,000 and a three tier system of decentralized institutions was introduced. The 74,000 communes expanded to 700,000 brigades; the 700,000 brigades further expanded to 5 million production teams with each team comprising only 20 households. The rationale for the division and subdivision was fairly obvious. The entire effort was to evolve a simple and rudimentary structure (the production team) so that people could control and participate in all decisions and activities that touched their lives. At the same time each successively larger grouping was an administratively viable structure capable of undertaking projects which demanded a bigger organization, more manpower and more funds.[8]

The functions of a commune cover a broad range from agriculture and industry to social aid. Galbraith in *A Chinese Passage* describes a commune which, though not necessarily typical in all respects, illustrates the diversity of production common to other communes. The Hsu Hang People's Commune near Shanghai has 4,694 households, 20,500 inhabitants and 1,688 hectares (approximately 4,200 acres) of land. Although the amount of irrigated land is less than an acre per family, the total grain output in 1972 was over 12,000 kg a hectare—more than twice the 1957 level—giving the commune a grain surplus. Highly mechanized by Chinese standards, the commune produces rice, wheat, cotton, hogs as well as engaging in a variety of factory enterprises. Small factories turn out $ 2·7 (Y 5·4) million worth of goods annually, producing half the total revenue of the commune.[9] Myrdal and Kessle in writing about Liu Ling, a village in Yeman which they consider typical of Chinese rural life in 1969, refer to the social aid that the commune system offers. Without application, means test or investigation, each member of Liu Ling gets approximately 172 kg of grain per year as a basic right—some 43 kg less than the average annual consumption of one person.[10] The Tachai Brigade of approximately 440 people has been hailed as a model of service to the people since 1964 for its endeavors in agriculture, irrigation and flood control. Tachai has popular symbolic importance for the Chinese because it represents the principles of the revolution, which stresses self-reliance at the commune, brigade and county levels and places emphasis on the role of women.[11]

The commune system provides a compromise between central planning and local control. Comprehensive planning is done at the commune level while the details of production and remuneration lie within the domain of the production teams. Decentralization permits an effective delivery of service locally, offering to the typical commune member, for instance, medical care of a higher caliber than is common in most places.

THE KIBBUTZIM OF ISRAEL

The kibbutzim owe their origin to youth groups eager to establish institutions on the basis of socialist ideology and in which the principle 'from each according to his ability to each according to his need' would be operative. The goal was a classless society with common ownership of the means of production to combat the social injustice of economic power. Conscious that in a technological age bureaucrats tend to concentrate power in their hands and that they can frustrate the aim of equality even in a system of common ownership, the pioneers of the kibbutzim promoted a direct democracy in which all the people would participate through the rotation of jobs and functions.

Within the kibbutz all aspects of living—work, recreation, family life, education—are regulated. The body having the right to decide such matters is the 'general assembly.' The assembly, however, is more than a representative body; it is made up of all members of the kibbutz. The functions of the assembly range from admission of new members to overall policy decisions. A member can bring to the assembly any item for discussion. The final decision on any matter is arrived at by a majority vote or some other formula the assembly uses to conduct its business.

A secretariat is elected to serve as the executive arm of the assembly. But, within the secretariat, offices rotate to prevent the substance and trappings of individual power. The secretariat, responsible for kibbutz administration, functions through various committees such as the education committee or the health committee. In addition, managers are elected to oversee work in agriculture, industry, animal husbandry, and the like. No one person can occupy any position—whether in the secretariat, on a committee or in management—beyond a particular term. Job rotation is the rule.

The kibbutzim of Israel are a good example of a people's institution. They provide individuals and families with food, shelter, recreation, education, health facilities, a sense of belonging, and security. Every person works and is entitled to all benefits. In old age or sickness a member is not deprived of his livelihood nor does he have to change his life style. The principle 'from each according to his ability to each according to his need' is operative and seems to work quite well. This is not to imply that the kibbutz does not have its stresses and strains. However, as models of decentralized institution building, the kibbutzim have withstood the test of time (the first one was set up in 1910) and they continue to function well within the Israeli society, based though it is on principles of individualism, competition and free enterprise. The kibbutzim have not only provided a way of life cherished by their members but they have also contributed significantly to the overall economy of Israel. The productivity of kibbutz industry is generally higher than that of the private sector.[12]

SUMMARY

Decentralized institution building is a way of ensuring that those affected by modernization have a voice in shaping their destiny. In those countries whose citizens previously took pride in democratic representation, there is now some clamor for participatory democracy. The term participatory democracy is applied to those decision making structures which follow basic democratic procedural norms such as majority rule, yet which extend equality through grassroots activity. Participatory democracy connotes decentralization of power by means of the 'direct involvement of amateurs' in authoritative decision making.[13] Social and economic progress is out of the question in developing countries without active citizen participation and control. Decentralized institution building provides the mechanism of involvement. The masses in developing countries cannot endure indefinitely their disillusionment with government bureaucracies or the realization of their own powerlessness in the hands of political and corporate leaders. Nor is discontent with the institutions of the establishment confined to the less developed world. Radical American economists, for instance, see the U.S. economy as primarily dominated by the monopolistic sector, consisting of corporate giants. They believe that the government acts to support class privilege and recreates it intergenerationally through the workings of its major institutions—education, health, the police, and the judiciary. From the radical perspective, reforms conceived within the existing institutions are inconsequential.[14] If social justice is to take the place of economic efficiency, the task facing society is to restructure old institutions and to build new ones.

NANCY RUNKLE HOOYMAN

8 Strategies of Citizen Participation

CITIZEN PARTICIPATION: A DILEMMA FOR SOCIAL DEVELOPMENT PRACTITIONER

The concept of citizen participation as an integral part of the development process has long been accepted as an ideal at the international level and is becoming accepted nationally in an increasing number of countries. The United Nations Declaration of Social Progress and Development states as a basic means for achieving social development that attention must be given to the 'adoption of measures to ensure the effective participation, as appropriate of all the elements of society in the preparation and execution of national plans and programs of economic and social development.'[1] The Second United Nations Development Decade affirmed that 'every effort will be made to secure the active support and participation of all segments of the population in the development process' and 'to make people aware of the benefits and sacrifices involved and to enlist their full participation in achieving the objectives of the decade.'[2] Citizen participation as either a goal of development or a means toward achieving development, or both, is a feature of a growing number of national plans. In fact, Almond and Verba maintain that 'if there is a political revolution going on throughout the world, it is what might be called the participation explosion.'[3]

Despite this emphasis on participation, the concept of citizen participation has not been clearly defined nor operationalized in most countries. As the Secretary-General's *Preliminary Report on a Unified Approach to Development Analysis and Planning* points out:

'Participation, like "planning", is sometimes treated as a mystical entity that will resolve problems once rightly conceived and applied.'[4] The practical implications of participation for development must be assessed in order to affirm for what purposes and under what conditions it can be a useful strategy.

One of the dilemmas frequently facing social development practitioners is between 'top-down' planning aimed toward specific goals and people's immediate needs versus grassroots 'bottom-up' organizational efforts intended to enable citizens to develop their own problem solving abilities over time. Much of the social development and community development literature describes this dilemma as one between what seems rational to planners versus what seems relevant to citizens.

Referring to the dialectic between the oppressor and the oppressed, Friere maintains that project sponsors in developing countries need to work with rather than for the oppressed.[5] Grosser contends that the issue of citizen self-determination versus governmental control is a major problem of the Welfare State.[6] Van Til and Van Til conceptualize the conflict as one between the citizen and the technically expert civil servant, who are both trying to influence government officials within a democratic setting. They define the critical challenge to social policy to be the development of mechanisms to accommodate the poor's interests without arousing the non-poor's power against them in a manner which stalemates change.[7] In his study of 54 American community decision organizations, Warren documented that most community planning bodies attempt to limit citizen participation to involvement by 'responsible' citizens who can act only through formalized channels; planning units tend to be opposed to citizen action or power.[8] Benz maintains that planners tell citizens what they want to hear, regardless of what the planners really intend to do; such planning is paternalistic, done for the people, not by the people.[9] Edlestone and Kolodner conclude that 'either time, money and method be available to facilitate a process which is more than perfunctory, or the pretense should be dropped altogether and program planning left to the technicians. Any course between is meaningless ritual.'[10] Two critical social development questions are thus inextricably linked: What is the boundary between professional and citizen prerogatives in bureaucratic governance and administration? What is the role of citizen-controlled community organization versus planning by experts as strategies to institutional change?

This conflict has emerged in various practice settings, for example, under the office of Economic Opportunity and Model Cities Programs in the United States in the 1960s and in many government-sponsored community development programs in developing countries. While the powerful and powerless both echoed the slogans of 'maximum feasible participation,' 'partnership,' and 'widespread participation' during the War on Poverty, the outcome in the majority of American cities was that citizens were not directly involved in planning or policy making.[11] Instead, the approach to citizen participation was often a 'top-down' means to obtain citizens' approval of professionally initiated plans. An adversary relationship frequently developed between citizens and those presumed to have technical expertise, whether as planners, researchers, or policy makers.

In developing countries, citizen participation has generally assumed a *status quo* orientation, which favors the already privileged groups—clearly the antithesis of what is intended when one considers the concept of development. For example, a program to build rural feeder roads through community self-help may, in effect, be of greatest benefit to large landowners and economic middlemen. Likewise, government funds 'saved' through the use of self-help techniques may be used to help finance industrialization which benefits the existing entrepreneurial class. Broadly speaking, from government's point of view, participation usually connotes contributing to development; from the citizens' perspective, participation generally means sharing in the political and economic development. These different perspectives open up the possibility of disagreement and antagonism.[12]

ARGUMENTS FOR AND AGAINST PARTICIPATION

Those with expertise generally express some or all of the following arguments against citizen participation. Citizens, especially those who are poor, are defined as lacking the knowledge, perspective and experience to contribute meaningfully to public decisions. In fact, it is argued that if the poor knew what was good for them, then they would not be poor. Since planners presumably know best how to solve a community's problems, professionally provided services are assumed to be an adequate substitute for a community's own problem solving efforts. Citizen participation is perceived as conflicting with representative forms of government and with long-range planning objectives; likewise, it presumably causes planning delays and interclass and interracial conflicts. In developing countries, especially in those that are newly independent, component groups may lack a clear vision of national goals or a national future. Instead, groups tend to view development in terms of their local or individually felt needs, involving an orientation to their present day situation and alleviation of current problems quickly. For example, in India, national leaders favored construction of large-scale dams in a few places while localities supported a network of small-scale irrigation works on individual farms. Similar cases of conflicts between long-term and short-term solutions abound in other countries.

In contrast, advocates of citizen power criticize administrative sponsorship of participation as manipulation,[13] a 'put-off strategy,'[14] cooptation,[15] and an educational-therapeutic approach toward 'problem' individuals and families.[16] Yet those who demand citizen power are often unable to define the conditions and strategies to attain it. Few practitioners have successfully developed effective organizational structures to insure meaningful participation or the mechanisms to provide citizens with the skills to deal constructively with complex technical problems. Thus, those who advocate involving the people-being-planned-for in the planning process are often unable to specify how.

This analysis aims to move beyond the slogans of 'people power' to suggest a model which integrates community organization, planning and research as strategies to attain substantive participation on a local or regional level. In doing so, past strategies and definitions of citizen participation are criticized.

A CONCEPTUAL FRAMEWORK

The conflict between 'top-down' planning and 'grass-roots' citizen participation can be conceptualized in terms of the sociological perspective of bureaucracy-primary group relationships. We have noted how differences of opinion regarding the power of the bureaucracy and the primary group have resulted in both cooptation and conflict between citizens and agencies in various planning efforts. In contrast, this analysis aims to present a model for an ongoing partnership between bureaucracies and primary groups, based on mutual respect for the importance of the separate roles of professionals and citizens.

Primary groups are characterized by non-instrumental, diffused relationships and face-to-face contact. For purposes of this analysis, the primary group is conceptualized as composed of citizens, whether as consumers, neighborhood residents, or agency clients. Citizens are defined as members of a community whose major source of power is through their own numbers, not through formal position, trained expertise, or money. Citizens have frequently been interpreted to mean low income groups and ethnic minorities.[17] While most of this analysis will be most relevant to social development situations involving professionals and low income minority groups, many points are applicable to the participation experiences of all citizens. The bureaucracy in most social development situations would be a human service delivery agency, a planning body, or a government unit, e.g., organizations in which trained technical expertise and large-scale resources are concentrated.

According to several urban sociologists, bureaucracy-citizen conflicts occur because bureaucracies have increased in size, importance, and extent of resources, while the primary group has declined in functions (Parsons, Simmel, Wirth, Marcuse). The bureaucracy is defined as the optimal structure for solving problems in our complex technological society. When such a theoretical perspective has been implemented, citizens have usually been defined—whether intentionally or inadvertently—as powerless, ignorant or apathetic, lacking the resources and expertise to decide about issues affecting them. Bureaucratic officials have relegated citizens to an advisory or review role and claimed that transferring any of their expertise to citizens would be inefficient. A self-fulfilling prophecy has usually resulted, with citizens viewing themselves as powerless and relying upon professionals.

Another sociological perspective, which forms the basis for many of the points made in this analysis, is that both the primary group and the bureaucracy have their own areas of expertise. Citizen groups are most efficient for dealing with unpredictable, idiosyncratic matters, value issues, or areas where knowledge is so sparse that experts cannot be trained. Bureaucracies are best for handling repetitive tasks that require routinization and large scale resources. In order for each to attain their goals, they need to cooperate, rather than experts seeking to control a citizen or citizens aiming to disrupt bureaucratic functions.[18] This analysis will suggest ways in which experts and citizens can cooperate to develop programs and policies to meet citizens' needs.

DEFINITION OF CITIZEN PARTICIPATION

While it is generally accepted that participation in a broad sense is 'good,' disagreement exists about what kind of voice citizens should have, in what aspects of a planning process, and with what degree of influence. Accordingly, citizen participation has been variously defined as forming membership on boards, attending meetings, advising community leaders, being employed through community development funds, voting, belonging to voluntary associations or clubs, holding office, serving with civic groups, and lobbying. The term participation has been used in such diverse contexts as self-help community development and particular institutional arrangements, such as village councils and cooperatives, worker representation in industrial management, political and social democracy and popular revolution. In fact, this variety of definitions creates a basis for many of the criticisms of participatory efforts, since in many cases participation has been merely an empty ritual or an end in itself, without significantly improving the quality of people's lives. The distribution of community power and resources has not been altered. Accordingly, as Arnstein notes, 'I participate, you participate, he participates, they profit.'[19]

In this analysis, citizen participation is defined as the process whereby citizens (e.g., people with only the power of their numbers) are able to actively exercise influence over significant decisions at different levels regarding societal goals and the allocation of resources and therefore the community's quality of life. Quality of life refers to the fact that problems in varied substantive areas are so interrelated that solutions in one area cannot be pursued without taking into account their effect on the community as a whole. This definition includes citizens' ability to extend their policy making role beyond the traditional act of voting to become involved on an ongoing basis in bureaucratic public decision making. Any citizen participation strategy should enable people to act upon whatever they perceive to be in their self-interest, whether it be housing, health, youth services or industrial development, and thus to contribute to something which they helped to define. Such citizen participation strategies are oriented toward social change, not toward system maintenance.

Citizen participation is not an end in itself, but a means to optimize the fit between programs, policies, and people's needs, through a redistribution of decision making power and resources. Since it is a means to resource distribution, participation is likely to be resisted by those with power. While participation may also be *an* end, since all people should have a right to participate in the decisions which affect their lives, it is not *the* end. The end is always equality, social justice, the abolition of poverty—in sum, an improved quality of life for all citizens. Admittedly, actions other than participation may be desirable in some circumstances; but practitioners must resolve the dilemma between 'top-down' and 'bottom-up' approaches in order to determine which actions are necessary and optimal to attain particular social development objectives. In other words, practitioners must distinguish whether participation is a means by which society can induce people to perform assigned tasks better or a means to which they can consciously alter their own tasks and therefore their societies.

Community organization is a means to citizen participation, and cannot be separated from it. Citizen participation enables community organizing to remain dynamic, while the organizing process gives direction to people's needs. By creating a sense of community, organizing enables people to develop their problem solving capabilities and to strike at the roots of systemic problems, rather than relying upon professionals who may deal only with the apparent symptom. The professional organizer thus plays a critical role in mobilizing citizens to take united action.

RATIONALE FOR CITIZEN PARTICIPATION

Proponents of citizen participation need to specify what they want citizens to participate in and why. This author's argument for citizen participation in bureaucratic public decision making is based on three major assumptions:

1. that citizen participation is a democratic right;
2. that social justice is most likely to be attained when all citizens can effectively voice their interests;

3. that informed citizens must be involved in the governance of bureaucracies in order to maintain institutions responsive to changing societal needs.

1. *Democratic Right*

The basic tenet of a democratic form of government is that power flows from the free will of each individual and is joined through a compact to create the will of the community. People are elected to carry out the wishes of those who give the power. While the democratic argument may be more the ideal than the practice, it nevertheless provides a unique basis for substantive participation through local citizen organizations and suggests that citizen participation is a necessary procedure to follow in formulating policies and plans.

This is also consistent with the democratic as opposed to the technocratic model of development. The democratic model holds that development, in order to be a socially responsible and effective enterprise, requires increasing participation by the people affected; political power must therefore be shared and administration decentralized. While the technocratic model concentrates power at the top, the democratic model distributes power by stipulating that citizens participate in the making of decisions that affect them.

Any democracy faces the problem of how to involve people in public decision making. Traditional popular ideology encourages voting for leaders and then relying on them. Some argue that direct participation is contrary to a representative form of government and delays decision making.[20] Yet reliance upon elected representatives can create feelings of powerlessness and leave needs unmet. Every representative serves such a wide variety of groups and interests that most individuals feel they have little effect on what is done. The ability of citizens to derive pride and self-respect from dealing actively with their own problems is assumed to be a critical element in an improved quality of life. This does not mean that public leaders relinquish the decision making responsibilities for which they are accountable, but that citizens also have the opportunities to define and create solutions to their problems. Such participatory opportunities are an affirmation of democracy. Some groups of citizens, however, may lack the organizational know-how to utilize these opportunities effectively. In such situations, organizational resources and training need to be provided to citizens who may not be affiliated with any institutions rather than merely coordinating the efforts of existing community organizations.

2. *Social Justice*

As noted, this author defines citizen participation as a means to ends, one of which is social justice. Presently, elected leaders are generally confronted by lobbyists, special interest groups, and the media, who have the resources to influence the governmental process. Leaders have difficulty knowing whether such influences represent only a small segment of the community or whether the interests are more broadly shared. The outcome is an unequal distribution of resources and power. In order to derive significant benefits from the political process, citizens must be able to participate in that process and compete effectively for a limited supply of rewards and benefits.[21] New institutional forms are necessary to represent the interests of low-income classes and to build those interests into the larger political and social structure.

Some contend that the organization of low-income persons increases class and racial polarization, because scarce resources prevent everyone from having a 'piece of the pie.'[22] However, this author assumes that when citizens are able to influence bureaucracies to be responsive to their interests, they are most likely to support political decisions essential to the well-being of all groupings in society. While the organization of the poor could be at the expense of other groups, issues and programs conducive to structural change can improve the quality of life for all people, such as minimum wage legislation, national health insurance, and environmental programs. A healthy pluralism may exist when citizen organizations can make positive, not merely negative, demands of public institutions.

3. *Informed Citizens and Institutional Responsiveness*

This author contends that citizens can make rational, informed decisions in allocating resources among competing priorities and demands. Involvement of informed citizens is assumed to bring to government officials definitions of needs and programs which would not otherwise be heard. Citizens are thus viewed as a source of special knowledge. While professionals may treat only the symptoms or 'felt needs,' citizens who live with the problems are better able to attack their source. Thus, the issue is not whether citizens can be trusted to make decisions, but how the decision making process can be structured to improve the likelihood that decisions made with citizens' input will be reached deliberately and carefully.

Institutional leaders also benefit from increased participation. Public decisions are more likely to be voluntarily accepted when people have been involved in them and are aware of the capabilities and limits of governmental institutions in delivering services. When ongoing mechanisms exist for citizen participation, officials have better access to citizen opinions. Thus, it is assumed that both citizens and institutional leaders can benefit from improved mechanisms for participation. For example, in one African country, government leaders and technicians decided to launch a major campaign to increase agricultural production and generate rural employment opportunities through the creation of new communal farms. This program was initiated without major participation by its intended beneficiaries. However, after several years of operation, relatively few people were willing to join the program, the new farms had low productivity, and the program had helped generate opposition to the government by the people. An evaluation of the program indicated that the major error in the program was the failure to consult with people prior to embarking on it. In other African countries, extensive use of *animation rurale* prior to making a decision about similar programs has increased citizen acceptance of the program and therefore its impact.[23]

Obstacles to Citizen Participation

The obstacles to citizen participation can be classified as internal, interpersonal, and external. Strategies to increase citizen involvement must take account of these obstacles.

I. INTERNAL OBSTACLES TO PARTICIPATION

Internal obstacles, which tend to be most characteristic of low-income groupings, lie within people's belief systems and within the resources which they have available for participation.

Belief Systems

Belief systems are conceptualized as how people view their life conditions and the manner in which they define events to be problems.[24] In turn, their problem definitions affect their potential for involvement. When people define problems in individual terms or 'blame the victim,' they are unlikely to join with others to try to effect change.[25] If they act at all, they tend to react against individuals and propose individualized rather than group solutions. For example, in a study of working class whites in four United States midwestern cities, this author found an association between blaming individuals for problems and acting along. Joining with others was not viewed as a potential solution to problems.[26] Warren also notes an individualistic, incremental approach to problems among Americans who are socialized to view society as basically sound and professional technologies as capable of resolving social problems.[27]

Citizens' values and sense of efficacy are components of belief systems which particularly affect their participation. An organizer must be aware of what is most important to people in their daily lives; in turn, strategies must be adapted in terms of these value systems, rather than attempting to change them. For example, family and occupational obligations may be more salient to lower and working class people than a norm of participation.[28] Accordingly, strategies might need to be structured to include family members and not to interfere with their work roles or schedules.

In his cross-cultured studies, Rogers has extensively documented the necessity for agents of community development to take account of the values and beliefs of a culture. Failure to do so increases people's alienation from decision makers. In turn, when only technical aspects of projects are considered, they are prone to failure.[29] For example, in one Latin American country, the national administrators decided to construct windmills to solve a water problem. The planning did not take into account the sociocultural milieu. The windmill became a focus of popular resentment and was ultimately destroyed by local peasants. Since no one had explained the windmill's purpose or function, it was interpreted as evil by people in their socioreligious context. Similarly, in a housing scheme in an African city, a standard European architectural plan was implemented primarily on technical grounds, and failed to consider the nature of African extended families. As a result, the turnover rate was high in the rehousing area and the highly valued family structure was impaired.[30] Bringing people into the decision making process and taking account of their value systems could have helped predict such possible difficulties, if not eliminate them.

Inefficacy includes the feeling that one cannot influence outside events and this acts as a barrier to participation. As the size, impersonality, and complexity of public bureaucracies have increased, community groups, particularly in low income areas, have felt increasingly powerless toward the political system.[31] By discouraging political participation, inefficacy further reinforces the poor's conditions of powerlessness.[32] Feelings of political inefficacy are not, however, limited to the poor. In the United States, the Senate Subcommittee of Intergovernmental Relations noted in 1973 that the 'growing trend of public opinion toward disenchantment with government swept more than half of all Americans with it.' In the 1973 Harris Study, more than one-half of Americans felt that the 'people running the country don't really care what happens to you;' two-thirds believed that 'what you think doesn't count any more.'[33] Such feelings of powerlessness may be expressed as acquiescence,[34] resignation, disengagement, protest,[35] or reliance upon professionals, which are major barriers to citizen pariticipation.

Resources

The resources necessary for participation can be classified as time, personnel, money, and knowledge of organizations and/or policy making procedures. Participation tends to require time away from family, friends, and work; if it entails attending numerous meetings and 'actions' or contributing dues, it can be an additional financial burden on citizens. Because of bureaucratic complexity, citizens need access to specialized knowledge to intervene effectively. Such knowledge is increasingly crucial with the shift from decision making grounded in politics to expertise, which has changed the 'rules for exercising power, as well as the structure of effective power;'[36] planning decisions, in particular, are cast in the context of abstract, technical analysis.

Availability of resources is affected by the family values and structure, such as income, interpersonal ties, and occupation, and by the neighborhood values and structure, such as the extent of formal-informal organization and racial and class homogeneity-heterogeneity. Obviously, low-income families and neighborhoods generally have few resources for participation, partially because of their limited experiences with bureaucratic decision making and their occupational and family demands. Piven documents that the poor have less organizational skill, less professional expertise, and fewer personal relations with officials than other classes.[37] As Lazar notes, 'most poor people don't belong to groups, don't go to meetings, don't express themselves in public.'[38] When people are pre-occupied with their immediate, basic needs, attending meetings may be an imposition upon them, especially when the meetings become ends in themselves without any significant alteration in their life conditions.

To minimize participation as an imposition, any attempts to increase involvement must assess the citizens' available resources and develop participatory strategies consistent with their resource base. Strategies should be physically accessible, flexible in terms of scheduling, and low in terms of psychic and financial costs. For example, a policy board or advisory committee approach would probably be an ineffective strategy in an area composed of many large families with scarce financial resources and limited knowledge of policy making roles, fathers holding physically exhausting jobs and mothers working, because participation on a board or committee requires a time commitment, knowledge of how bureaucracies operate, money to pay costs incurred such as babysitting and transportation and perhaps time off from work. *Ad hoc* voluntary associations would be a strategy more consistent with the limited resource base and therefore, more likely to succeed and to be a means to increase low-income citizens' resources.

The internal obstacles to participation are thus an orientation toward individualistic blame and incremental change; the low saliency of participation in most value systems; feelings of inefficacy and resignation; and limited knowledge and financial resources. Strategies of participation must be structured to minimize these internal obstacles; yet the emphasis must be on developing participatory mechanisms that meet people 'where they're at,' rather than an educational-therapeutic approach which 'blames the victim' and aims to modify citizens' values. Once citizens do participate in structures that impact on the quality of their life conditions, some of these internal obstacles are likely to be diminished.

II. INTERPERSONAL OBSTACLES TO PARTICIPATION

Interpersonal obstacles lie in citizens' interactions with others, either with peers or 'superiors,' such as government officials or higher-income people.

Expectations of others and the functional relevancy of participation are critical interpersonal factors among peers. Participation is unrewarding when family and friends do not value it. For example, in the United States OEO programs, 'there seemed to be little prestige derived from (CAP Board) membership and little opportunity to satisfy a constructive sense of power.'[39]

Participation on boards which are socioeconomically representative is generally not rewarding for low-income people, since they feel looked down upon and uncomfortable with higher status members. Edelstone and Kolodner note that low-income residents' 'resistance to broadening the participation was clearly based on fear of domination by those who were more technically informed and articulate about housing matters.'[40] However, by refusing to include people with more expertise in their meetings, these citizens cut themselves off from the technical assistance necessary to implement their plans.

Even differences in dress, gestures, and manner of speech can be threatening to citizens. For example, in this author's interviews with working class people, a resident claimed that he would not attend city-wide School Board meetings because he felt uncomfortable in his work overalls, although he was active in neighborhood meetings where other men wore work clothes.

These interpersonal obstacles imply the difficulty of forming coalitions between different socioeconomic and ethnic groups. When low-income or minority persons are uncomfortable in such interactions, middle class domination is likely. It appears necessary to first organize the different groupings separately before attempting to form coalitions between them that are based on their common interests.

III. EXTERNAL OR STRUCTURAL OBSTACLES TO PARTICIPATION

Organizers and planners need to take account of such internal and interpersonal obstacles to participation. However, focussing solely upon them can lead to educational-therapeutic-cooptative techniques, where the professionals view their role as one of informing citizens and allowing them to react to already formulated plans. Yet the major obstacles to participation appear to be external, lying outside the citizen's control of his daily life circumstances.

An analysis of external obstacles requires examining the manner in which programs, policies, and plans are structured to minimize substantive citizen participation in decision making, even though lip service may be given to the concept of involvement. In terms of our conceptual framework, the bureaucracy generally reaches out to the primary group or community, or 'reaches down' to the 'client served'; it initiates and thereby controls the conditions of participation.

Such bureaucratically-defined participation was especially common in the United States during the Urban Renewal Programs of the 1950s, but has also continued under the Poverty Programs and Model Cities of the 1960s and the Goals Programs, Community Development Act, and the programs for regionalism-decentralization in the 1970s. While little city halls and neighborhood-based services are physically closer to the people, the structures for involvement nevertheless tend to be imposed from the top-down. Thus, the basic anamoly of such bureaucratic outreach efforts is that decisions regarding whether citizens shall participate or not, the time period when they will be involved, their areas of discretion, and their options for action are made by legislators, administrators, and planners, e.g., by those who possess the power of position, money or trained expertise, not by the citizens. Citizens are thus put in the role of reactors, not initiators. The power-holders, by setting the conditions for participation in programs and policies, are proposing to 'give' people limited power, even though power in a democratic setting originally came from the people. This model for involvement overlooks the fact that citizen power, grounded in the American democratic tradition, is not an extremist demand. Yet, in many cases, power-holders are only willing to implement some type of minimal participation in order to obtain Federal Government funds.

In developing countries, bureaucracies have often controlled the conditions for participation under the guise of community development programs. While many community development programs have provided essential resources to low-income communities, they nevertheless have tended to limit participation to passive rather than active forms. In other words, people have merely endorsed decisions made for them, or only helped implement decisions about which they were not consulted. A review of community development projects in Latin America indicates that local people were mobilized primarily to provide material resources and labor power for improvement projects, not to take part in shaping a program or criticizing its content. In such Latin American self-help projects, participation tended to be viewed as an action technique rather than a basic objective implying structural changes in society.[41]

The most common roles, played by citizens as reactors to the top-down imposition of the conditions for participation, are:

1. The citizen as *recipient of information* concerning plans that have already been made by technical experts and political officials. Through public hearings, mass media techniques, and information and referral services, citizens participate as consumers of information. In some cases, they may be solicited for their opinions, such as door-to-door surveys, grievance procedures, or ombudsmen. Yet the bureaucracy often determines what will be done to this information. Generally, the bureaucracy is concerned with obtaining support for their current program goals, even when they are against the poor's material interests.[42] Studies of peasant participation in Columbia and Venezuela indicate that when peasants participated, they were more likely to internalize norms which supported legitimate power; participation therefore benefitted the national leaders.[43] Political expediency thus frequently underlies officials' apparent concern for participation.

2. The citizen as *opinion leader*, who links public agencies and individuals or families who need services. This service-oriented approach assumes that programs and policies are basically adequate; what is necessary is that more people be aware of and use these services or that citizens be involved in planning for incremental improvements in services, under the professionals' guidance. Rogers emphasizes that the community development agent should work with local opinion leaders in order to facilitate the diffusion of innovations throughout the local culture.

Another difficulty is that the opinion leader may become distant from the people he is presumed to represent. As Rogers documented in his cross-cultural studies, opinion leaders differ from their followers in terms of their social status and degree of innovativeness.[44] In the American Poverty Program, many presumed opinion leaders were unrepresentative of the program constituency; concerned with upward mobility, they served to legitimize the bureaucracy's intervention and to advance their own interests.[45]

3. The citizen as agency *paraprofessional staff* or *common messengers* between citizens and professionals. This strategy usually leads to conflict between the bureaucracy and the community primary group.[46] Paraprofessional contacts with their community groups have been minimized by their upward mobility and by their need to be loyal to their employers in order to retain job security.

4. The citizen as *advisor*, who serves on a policy board or advisory committee. While the American Model Cities Program did place some citizens in policy making roles, citizens' impact was limited by their being a numerical minority. Such boards were usually structured—and citizens selectively recruited—to support the agency's goals and were more procedural than participatory in nature.[47] The experts or officials continued to control the sources of power, such as information, budget, and staff. Similarly, in an examination of cooperatives in one Asian country, it was found that government officials frequently outnumbered local leaders two-to-one on secondary and tertiary planning and administrative bodies. This was a major factor in the unsuccessful performance of a number of cooperatives.[48]

When the bureaucracy defines participation, citizens are 'acted upon', but not allowed to initiate or encouraged to find alternatives to existing social institutions; only administrative involvement is attained, not substantive participation in the determination of policy.[49] In his study of community decision organizations throughout the United States, Warren documents such 'gross responsiveness,' where agencies provide for low-income participation in order to improve public relations or interpret their existing programs and policies to citizens. The people involved in decision making were not those who had to live with the decision outcomes.[50] Instead, citizens were defined as clients to be served, 'forced into the role of responding as selfish, dependent individuals.'[51]

Few structural changes have resulted from such bureaucratic participation. In 17 of the 20 Community Action Agencies studied by Austin in the United States, participation was operationalized to have organizational and advisory, not political, functions and a pattern of formal cooptation resulted. Even where citizens did form a policy making board, their budget was less than one hundred dollars, which prevented their effecting significant changes. Consequently, target area residents had little impact on the major program strategies. Austin concluded that the system was structured to prevent meaningful participation.[52] Warren's analysis of community decision organizations in the American Model Cities Program also found changes only in superficialities, not in the core activities.[53] Regarding both programs, Aleshire concludes that decentralization of power cannot be successfully administered by a system which is not prepared to support change.[54]

Likewise, in Latin American countries, the government may deliberately attempt to promote or control citizen organizations, depending upon how compatible they are with the State. Organizations, such as the unions of urban workers, have received close attention in the form of a shifting combination of encouragement and regulation from the highest levels of political leadership, primarily because of the importance of including such organizations in given systems of political compromise. Other organizations, such as unions of rural workers, have been practically outlawed. This is understandable within the national content in which these organizations and the systems of land tenure are incompatible, and landowners are very powerful within systems of political compromise. Likewise, some forms of organizational action will be accepted more readily than others by the authorities, with the state supporting organized mutual aid and punishing strikes and civil disobedience.[55] The extreme of such control is when participation is punished by death, as in La Compamento in Chile. The end result is that the political economic system basically remains unchanged.

Similarly, the 'Panchayat' in India was created as part of a scheme to promote rural development, without offering any explicit challenge to existing property or power and caste relationships. As the United Nations evaluation team noted in the late 1950s, despite all the efforts of the community development teams, the poorer peasants still lacked incentives while the richer peasants and landlords were able to appropriate their surplus; thus social and economic divisions had actually widened.[56] In Africa, government-sponsored community development projects served to build up the economic infrastructure and discouraged unfavorable institutions and attitudes that might lead to the development of a radical challenge.[57]

When past citizen involvement efforts are examined in terms of the theory of bureaucracy-primary group relations, it is evident that administrators and planners have generally utilized strategies that are most effective for keeping citizens at a distance from their programs and for perpetuating an unfriendly or hostile relationship, not for substantially involving citizens. Techniques of mass media, public hearings, common messengers, policy and advisory boards, and working through other organizations are a means to minimize meaningful citizen participation in bureaucratic decision making, because they do not allow sufficient face-to-face communication or primary group intensity and focussed expertise. In other words, opportunities for two-way communication, for feedback, for developing trust, and for interpretation of information are absent.[58] Yet interpersonal contact is essential when the message—the program or plan being communicated to citizens—is complex and when citizens are hostile or indifferent to the bureaucracy. As concluded by one of the Commissions on Citizen Participation at the XVIIth International Conference on Social Welfare, 'participation is not possible without the organization of constant exchange between the grassroots communities and the higher echelons. It is particularly necessary for two-way communication to be ensured, from the grassroots to the top of the hierarchy and from the top of the hierarchy to the grassroots.'[59]

Most past programs have also failed to provide intensive training which would enable citizens to comprehend complex technical information in order that they could act upon it.[60] Little attempt has been made even to confirm that citizens were understanding what they were voting on.[61] In the United Kingdom, for example, the Skeffingtom report on local participation in planning noted that planners had frequently not succeeded in conveying information to the people.[62] Distance maintaining techniques such as mass media further limit participation by controlling the source and flow of information which citizens receive. In fact, the board members of Community Action Programs (CAP) in the United States were 'lucky if they were able to see a program proposal 48 hours in advance.'[63] Citizens on CAP Boards experienced difficulty in reviewing plans or initiating proposals because of the projects' technical nature and the staff's failure to provide adequate information and technical assistance.[64] Because citizens did not have the technical expertise, their involvement lengthened the time of program planning and implementation, which in turn increased planners' resistance to citizen input and citizens' mistrust and hostility toward professionals tended to grow.

In terms of our conceptual framework, the distance between the bureaucracy and the community-primary group increased because inappropriate participatory strategies were used. When such distance maintenance links are used to limit information and to present complex materials without any explanation, citizen participation efforts seem doomed to failure. Critics of participation can then point to their failure to confirm their belief that citizens are unqualified to participate in decision making.

When citizens receive goals rather than set them and attend endless meetings rather than form a broad base of decision making, participation can become a burden imposed upon them, not a right. Under such conditions, low-income citizens appear to be required to participate to attain some life conditions that other socioeconomic groupings already enjoy and to support the existing political-economic systems. The poor are mandated to display a different pattern of participation than the nonpoor. In such situations, participation is inconsistent with the objectives of social development, since it does not lead to either the individual's increased dignity, an improved quality of life or structural modifications of the society.

COMMUNITY INTERVENTION IN BUREAUCRACIES

Perhaps partially in reaction to the frustrations of bureaucratic-initiated participation and as a result of rising citizen expectations, citizens in a variety of settings have organized outside the normal political channels against bureaucracies, which they define as the 'enemy.' Such actions take the form of demonstrations, boycotts, civil disobedience and revolution and are often initiated by students, workers, ethnic minorities and increasingly women. These forms of direct and oftentimes spontaneous citizen participation continue to break out in both the developing and the developed world, without regard to the existing social system or form of government.

The sit-ins, pickets, strikes, and boycotts in the United States in the 1960s alerted authorities to the existence of problems and brought some incremental gains to citizens or consumer groups, such as welfare mothers or low-income tenants. Student uprisings in Thailand and Greece were instrumental in overthrowing the government. However, the citizen as social activist is often in a reactive or defensive position, responding to a threat to their interests rather than initiating alternative policies to benefit citizens in their areas. The outcome of such confrontations may be a total renunciation of the plan by the technicians, a breakdown in the delivery of needed social services, or suppression of citizens' demands, rather than any attempt to collaborate in planning to meet the needs of both parties. Thus, while direct citizen action can at time yield benefits, under other circumstances it may actually hinder social progress and development and entail extremely high costs, such as loss of life or property.

Citizens have also been limited in their protests against bureaucracies by their lack of technical resources and knowledge required to be effectively involved in decisions about bureaucratic policies and programs. Through disruptive tactics, citizens may initially get the bureaucracy's attention, but be unable to sustain any long-term involvement. Bureaucracies have frequently responded to protests with symbolic rewards rather than substantive changes.[65] For example, in the Harlem (New York City) rent strike in 1963–64, the strike leader lacked administrative and financial skills and was unable to define movement goals on a citywide basis. As a result, short-term 'emergency' changes were made, but the basic conditions of tenement existence remained unaltered.[66]

In many such cases, citizens have only the power of their numbers. The balance theory points out that 'people power' is sufficient to arouse initially the bureaucracy's attention (and, oftentimes, anger) to the group's demands, but it is inadequate to bring about long lasting changes in bureaucratic structure and function.[67] Such citizen groups need knowledge of the legislative and policy making processes and of bureaucratic structure to determine where to intervene to implement changes. When such knowledge resources are not indigenous to the group, then they need finances in order to be able to hire an advocate who has expertise and can consult with their groups or to form an advocate bureaucracy to represent them. Yet most citizen protest groups are *ad hoc* and lack such finances. For example, in his study of 52 neighborhood associations in ten areas throughout the United States, Austin found that all associations had limited financial resources.[68]

Another limitation of social action efforts has been their tendency to focus only on one issue and, accordingly, to be short-term and episodic. Thus, while people may actively work together, attend meetings and discuss issues for short periods of time, maintaining this level of participation over time is difficult, in the Harlem (New York City) rent strike, the housing committees did not continue beyond the strike's duration.[69] Austin determined that three-quarter of all action issues of the 52 neighborhood associations in the United States were focussed on environmental or service improvements specific to a single neighborhood.[70] Single issue groups may win immediate gains, but are unlikely to join with other organizations to form a powerful, ongoing citizen force. Promoting participation around only one project often means that once the project is completed, the incentive for participation disappears. In such cases, citizens may be manipulated by professional organizers as well as by planners, because of the organizer's failure to build slowly and carefully an ongoing, stable citizen organization.

Social action tactics also have the effect of increasing polarization between professionals and citizens. Even when professionals have assumed advocacy roles, 'little has been accomplished without the most painful kind of controversy and furor.'[71] An adversary relationship has often developed, with citizens distrusting the planners and planners devising means to circumvent governmental requirements for participation. In fact, while planners may have coopted citizens, citizens themselves have undertaken a manipulative strategy of protest against established institutions.[72] In some situations, a backlash has occurred, with planners refusing to have anything to do with citizen groups, even to the point of not undertaking the minimum of public hearings. In such an adverse situation, neither party wins and the quality of life remains unchanged.

A BALANCE THEORY APPROACH TOWARD CITIZEN PARTICIPATION

Advocates of disruptive intervention in bureaucracies thus fail to recognize that planners do possess some legitimate skills and functions which citizens do not have. On many complex, technical, social and economic problems, citizens lack the necessary trained expertise. It can be an abuse of their individual dignity to involve them in such complex problem solving efforts without providing them with the necessary technical expertise and information resources. In some situations, planners do have a legitimate basis for asking that citizens 'leave them alone' in order that they can complete their work. In other aspects of decision making, citizens

S. D.—10

who live with the problems have the right and the knowledge to be involved. Planners and organizers need to differentiate the areas of development requiring the planners' trained expertise and the citizens' particular knowledge and experience. As noted by a United Nations review of participatory efforts: 'In practice, the best approach may be a combination of an institutional structure which permits an adequate level of participation by popular representatives, based on a parity between technical requirements for decision-making for which local officials and technicians are given a decision-making role and socio-political requirements for which popular representatives are needed.'[73] The remainder of this analysis will present a model for collaboration between citizens and professionals, without either party dominating the other.

The proposed model rejects both bureaucratic-sponsored involvement and grassroots protest as the primary strategies to increase citizen participation. Instead, it draws upon the balance theory approach to social change, which maintains that both the bureaucracy and the citizens groups have legitimate spheres of influence, ideally suited to perform certain tasks, and therefore should collaborate in order to attain their goals.[74] This model also assumes that social development is an integrated approach to bringing about systemic change. In other words, professionals—whether they be planners, organizers, researchers, economists—need to work as a team in attacking local, regional, and national problems. Unfortunately, in the past, such professionals have all too often been in isolation from each other and, in some cases, in conflict with each other. Organizers have mobilized angry citizens against planners and communication has broken down. Citizen participation experiments have not been adequately evaluated nor research results shared, so that the 'wheel has had to be reinvented' each time government has legislated involvement. The technical skills of the economist, the researcher, or the planner have not been sufficiently available to citizens groups facing complex problems, such as pollution or unemployment. When they have been provided, they have been presented to citizens in a paternalistic manner.

This model thus seeks to avoid agency-sponsored participation, single-issue, *ad hoc* protest efforts, and a fragmented single discipline approach to community problem-solving. The major professionals to be involved are organizers, planners, researchers, and other resource people, such as librarians or teachers who would work as a team and aim to be responsive to citizen groups. Since these professionals would be part of a grassroots effort working from a community base rather than allied with existing programs or institutions, new alternative role definitions are necessary. These role changes are discussed below.

Any model for effective citizen participation must address two major problems faced in past efforts; the absence of effective structures for citizen participation in public decision making and citizens' lack of expert knowledge to enable them to solve complex technical problems.

STRUCTURE FOR CITIZEN PARTICIPATION

Partnership necessitates building *broad-based, multi-issue, grassroot, autonomous citizen organizations*; these will enable citizens to bargain on a more equal basis with professionals in formulating and implementing public policy, programs, and plans to resolve social and economic problems.

Building autonomous, self-help citizen organizations at the grassroots level can begin to resolve many of the difficulties faced by top-down approaches to participation. The underlying assumption is that organization is a means to power—in fact, the only viable means for low-income citizens who do not have the power of money and knowledge. As people experience success in an organization, they realize that united they can be more influential than they can be by acting individually or in small, *ad hoc* groups. Through their broad-based organization, citizens can be constructively involved in a wide variety of issues, depending upon their needs and perceptions.

A clear lesson from the American organizational experiences in the sixties is the need for a mass base rather than a minority base. The welfare rights movement, for example, was limited by the fact that no matter how many welfare mothers were organized, they remained a minority. Issues are needed that will unite low and moderate income people and people of different racial groups and pit them against their common enemies rather than against each other.

This multi-issue, multi-strategy approach is likely to be more long-lasting than single issue organizations are. Because it aims to involve all citizens within a defined, relatively small locality, it can minimize polarization within the community. Instead of providing services to those affected by the problem, or focussing on long-range, abstract objectives, professionals would work with citizens to eradicate the source of specific, definable problems in their community.

As a grassroot strategy, the focus is to involve ordinary citizens at the local level. Past citywide bureaucratic-sponsored efforts to involve 'representative' groupings have failed to take account of class differences in people's ability and willingness to participate and in the interests that motivate them to act. In social development efforts, it is necessary that low-income alienated people have as much ability to pursue their interests as do higher income organizationally sophisticated citizens. This requires that an organizer work intensely with small local groups to increase their skills, involvement and influence within a well defined community rather than with an entire community. Building block clubs and neighborhood organizations is a means to involve previously inactive individuals. In many countries, traditional forms of local participation have been used to revive earlier forms of indigenous participation, such as the barrio councils in the Philippines, the ujama's village in the context of African socialism and *animation rurale*. The traditions of popular participation at the local level and their revival indicate the potential viability of the process.[75]

Critics of this approach may contend that locally-based grassroots efforts do not lead to significant societal changes, since major decisions are generally made at the national level; however, such activities can modify local institutions that directly affect the participants and therefore are justified as social development efforts. In addition, local groups can be indirectly involved in regional and national decision making. In the United States, for example, local groups concerned with housing rehabilitation and unfair lending practices have joined together to form a national coalition (National People's Action) which impacts on federal legislation.

In order to maintain a citizen organization's autonomy, indigenous leadership must be developed, rather than citizens relying upon established leaders, such as elected officials. When established leaders are involved in organizational activities, citizens frequently show excessive deference to them. In order for citizens to develop confidence in their own problem solving capabilities, they need to be able to relate in an easy, relaxed manner to indigenous leaders whom they trust. The balance approach indicates the need to build stable organizations of ordinary citizens—those who may never before have been involved, who feel powerless and alienated—before citizens attempt to work with professionals. Considerable time must therefore be devoted to the process of slowly and carefully building an organization before citizens go to the bargaining table.

Sponsorship and the role of the professional organizer are critical issues to be addressed in building autonomous citizen organizations. The American OEO and Model Cities experiences and community development efforts in developing countries indicate the difficulties of bureaucracies legislating participation. While citizen participation cannot be effectively legislated or mandated by officials, it can be facilitated. And in many cases officials—whether within private foundations, religious organizations, or governmental units—want to develop new institutions for political involvement, but do not know how. They recognize that the present professional-citizen conflicts are undesirable, and they want to reduce citizen alienation. To achieve these goals, they have frequently turned not to government organizations but to private foundations and churches—partially for financial reasons and partially to protect their autonomy.

Professional staff working with neighborhood organizations face conflicts of loyalty between their citizen constituencies and their funding sources; Grosser suggests that organizers maintain their independence through the role of broker. He also emphasizes a low visibility staff role, that of primarily contributing knowledge of organizing techniques and bureaucracies.[76] In this proposed model, the organizer would also serve the important function of resource-linker. The organizer would link people with the resources of the researcher, the planner, or the teacher, for example, but would not tell them when to request such resources or how to use them. Obviously, the organizer's personality would be an important variable. Kahn describes a good organizer as one who is not egotistical; but who likes him or herself, who has a good sense of humor; who is well-balanced and able to relate to a variety of people, and has a respect for all people.[77]

One of the criticisms of *ad hoc* social action efforts has been that while citizens may be able to effect specific decisions, they cannot actually participate in their implementation. Thus, the role of the planner, researcher or other resource person is essential in enabling citizens to be involved at every stage of decision making. The balance theory points to the need to differentiate complex tasks which require professionals' trained expertise from idiosyncratic, policy, or value issues where citizens are experts. Such differentiation prevents participation from becoming a burden upon citizens. In other words, citizens would not be requested—as federal programs have frequently done—to perform tasks that are beyond their area of expertise or interest. As resource-linker, the organizer would invite the researcher to research the problems which people define as economic and social issues and to provide information in easily interpretable formats. Researchers would also evaluate various strategies as they are implemented in order to determine their effectiveness and would share the results with the citizen organization. The planner's role would be most important at the stage of formulating solutions and implementing them. The planner would work with citizen task groups to assist them in identifying needs and the most appropriate means of problem solving. This would include lending technical expertise in specific areas that are change targets as well as advising how to make certain that concessions from influential decision makers actually result in the outcomes desired by the citizen organization.

This critique of bureaucratic-sponsored participation has noted how citizens have not had sufficient opportunities to be involved in decisions that directly affect them. For example, citizens generally have had a haphazard review function toward plans; in turn, planners have feared (and, in some cases, legitimately so) that citizens would interfere with the technical aspects of their jobs. By contrast, in this approach, citizens must first mobilize their resources to achieve their own objectives rather than rely upon experts to do things *for* them. The citizen organization would seek professional advice and assistance only when it could not solve its own problems. This distinction is consistent with the balance theory assumption that both citizens and experts have legitimate spheres of influence. However, where knowledge is equal, citizen groups are structurally more efficient than bureaucracies because they can make decisions faster, more flexibly, and at a lower cost.[78]

While this author does not advocate that citizens take over professionals' jobs, citizens are assumed to have the capability to carry out tasks which do not necessarily require trained expertise: to identify local needs, to set goals and standards for community achievement, to participate in formulating public policy, to gather information on local issues, to be involved in overseeing the performance of local institutions, and to delegate to governmental and other community institutions the authority to perform the tasks best accomplished by them. In other words, citizens can decide *what* is to be done; professionals can then be charged with the responsibility for deciding *how* it will be done.

In addition to consulting with professionals, a citizen organization can serve a watch-dog function, finding out about potential problems, researching them before they occur, and taking appropriate action before it is too late. Once a citizen organization is ongoing and stable, it can be the bargaining agent for a neighborhood in its interactions with higher levels of decision making. Instead of bureaucracies 'reaching down' to the community, citizens would have the organizational and resource base to initiate collaboration with experts on their own terms.

Training for Citizen Organizations

This analysis has noted how citizens have in the past lacked the technical and informational resources to participate meaningfully in governmental decision making. Even when information has been public, participants may not have known where to find it and how to utilize it. As a result, citizens have often failed even to understand all sides of complex issues. Lacking understanding of the complexities facing professionals, they have tended to react angrily or simplistically, thus widening the communication gap between professionals and citizens. The American Poverty Program experience indicates that it is insufficient simply to provide citizens with expert consultants who possess the necessary information and who then tell citizens what their options are. Citizens need to be provided with information in a manner that allows them to internalize it. Then they will have the indigenous resources to understand how complex issues affect them, advocate realistic approaches to their resolution, and decide what further expertise they need to draw upon. The technique of *concientizacion* has been successfully used in Latin American countries, where the people visualize their problem situation and find their own solutions autonomously.

Professionals need to be able to transfer some of their skills to citizens in order to maximize citizens' problem-solving capabilities and to minimize over time the need for professional assistance.

While completing tasks is important, the discovery and development of indigenous leadership is even more essential. Every effort should be made at every stage to insure that most of the work is done by citizens and not by professionals, in order that citizens learn skills to solve problems in the future. As noted above, one way to implement this is for the organizer to link citizens with the necessary resources.

Many countries have worked to broaden the base for leadership through training new and generally younger leaders who can quickly learn the skills required for performing new institutional roles. In French-speaking Africa, *animation rurale* has sought to provide new leadership through training young villagers to act as *animateurs*. In Tanzania, the *ujama's* villages are in a large measure based on youth.

Another way to increase the knowledge resources available to citizen groups, especially in developed countries, is through information centers that furnish data for citizens to use in researching and acting on issues; such information would include research reports, census data, current legislation, and grant-writing materials. To insure that citizen organizations can effectively utilize the information, these centers would need to have a service-oriented, outreach approach. This orientation suggests, for instance, a new role for the professional librarian. Instead of waiting for citizens to request library services, the librarian would attend citizens' meetings, listen to their requests for information, and then follow up by providing the necessary materials. The librarian would also have to be willing to present data in a form which citizens could understand.

Training in specific substantive areas, such as health, economic development and pollution, is essential in order for citizens to be meaningfully involved in decision making. Citizens can acquire organizational skills from professional organizers. But they also need to acquire research and problem solving skills through locality-based training sessions or through attending regional and national conferences and workshops.

The Process of Building Citizen Organizations

The partnership model requires that the organizer have considerable autonomy from existing agencies and be able to select a community to organize which has a need and desire to participate.

The sponsoring organization should not dictate in advance what the target community should be. Instead the organizer should explore the potential for citizen organizations in a number of communities. Initially, the organizer could use existing data to identify communities facing economic and social concerns that might motivate people to united action in community-wide objectives. Kahn emphasizes the time and care that should be taken in entering a community.[79] In this model, the organizer would attempt to talk with both previously inactive citizens as well as identifiable leaders to assess people's concerns about community problems, their interest in and potential for ongoing action to deal with them, and their acceptance of the organizer's presence. In all cases, the organizer would only stay if the community agreed.

Agencies frequently rely upon standardized survey instruments to collect objective data about the community. Such data generally tell little about how citizens define problems to be issues, their perceptions of the problems' source, their belief systems, and the amount of resources which they have available for participatory efforts. For this reason, the organizer should utilize ethnographic techniques of observation and open-ended, conversational, in-depth interviews in which citizens are allowed to talk freely about their concerns. The balance theory suggests the value of the organizer's face-to-face contacts and working through indigenous opinion leaders as means to close the distance between citizens and professionals.[80] Such an approach allows for two-way communication and facilitates the internalization of information and the development of trust.

After reaching a fairly large and representative group of citizens, the organizer would meet with identifiable leaders to present to them the issues which emerged in the interviews and the possibilities for involving citizens in ongoing decision making. A steering committee would be formed. A written agreement would be developed to enumerate expectations for both the professionals and the community for a specific time period.

The next task would be to build an ongoing representative organization which translates individual needs into united efforts for community-wide objectives. In order to involve as many citizens as possible, considerable effort would be devoted to building block clubs and ongoing committees and to conducting a people's convention, where a constitution and by-laws would be adopted and officers elected. In building the organization, the organizer must attempt to develop tactics which do not place an excessive burden upon people's resource base. Such an approach might mean forming car pools, flexible scheduling, providing child care during meetings, choosing a site that is accessible and consistent with people's value sytems, and allowing some 'fun' and socializing during meetings and actions. In sum, the organizer must recognize internal and interpersonal obstacles to participation and modify any strategy to take account of them. The organizer must identify and then build upon and strengthen people's sense of community in order that the organizing process will be defined and led primarily by the people.

CONCLUSION

Only implementation will test the effectiveness of the partnership model and determine its cultural range and limitations. The research needed to evaluate the approach must encounter the obstacles facing all action research—interdisciplinary barriers which impede cooperation, and entrenched interests opposed to funding projects likely to upset the scales of community power. Despite the difficulty of redistributing influence, the partnership model has the advantage of taking into account simultaneously the internal, interpersonal and external impediments to citizen participation. The conflict of planner versus organizer, professional versus citizen can be minimized by suggesting a basis for collaboration, thus lessening the problem of professionals dominating citizens and citizens disrupting the efforts of professionals. Throughout the process, it is essential to emphasize that the goal of citizen participation is to improve the quality of life for all.

P. D. KULKARNI

9 Educational Policy and Planning

The history of education is almost as old as the history of civilization. The educational systems today in different countries of the world are the product of the cumulative wisdom of the ages. Yet the processes of articulating educational policies and formulating educational plans are of very recent origin. The industrialized countries of the world thought of it when they were reordering their lives after World War II. The developing countries, most of whom had only recently acquired their political independence, also began efforts in that direction in the 1950s when they launched their own national development plans. In other words, the history of educational policy and planning, as parts of official exercises in development planning, can be traced over three decades only.

MACROSCOPIC VIEW

Articulation of educational policies implied most of the following features; the precise combination varying from country to country or from time to time within the same country. In the first place, it implied viewing education as a whole, whether as a system or otherwise. It was a view through a wide-angle lens, encompassing the educational activities at all levels from the elementary to the highest and in the country as a whole. In most cases, this was the first ever macroscopic view of total education vertically and horizontally. Secondly, education was considered as part of the overall developmental strategy. In fact, as we shall presently see, the dictates of national development became in most instances the most important, if not the sole rider on educational policies and plans. Educational policy makers and planners began to take a long-term view of the educational process. In doing so, they had naturally to foresee the socioeconomic changes that would occur at progressive stages of development and their probable impact on educational needs and problems. To put it differently, new dimensions of education surfaced. The interaction between the demographic trends and their influence on the extent of educational need, manpower requirements progressively diversified and sophisticated, the pace and pattern of modernization of the economy are but a few of the examples of major new dimensions which became for the first time the concern of those responsible for educational policies and plans. Great public debates arose at the national and international levels on certain issues which question the very fundamentals of education. Controversies have not ceased even now but great advance has been made in asking the right questions. Some of the more important of those questions will be examined in the following paragraphs.

I. POLICY ISSUES

OBJECTIVES OF EDUCATION

Given the long history of education, one might expect clear consensus on the objectives of education, and some disagreement only on the manner of achieving them in the shortest possible time. Unfortunately, that is not so. Instead of possessing cogently formulated goals and objectives, most educators and policy makers rely on certain rough assumptions—the Gross Conceptual Product (G.C.P.), which goes as follows:

> Education is good, inherently so. In order to develop manpower required to usher in and sustain a modern economy education must spread among the large masses of people. It is a question of finding the financial, the material and the manpower resources to extend education universally. The only constraint on this is the lack of one or more of the triple resources and if only the required resources are furnished education will become a universal system pouring out its finished product (graduates) into the world.

Put it thus and it also looks more like a quantitative exercise; largely if not solely so. There is nothing wrong in dwelling upon the strategies of education but a more fundamental inquiry should precede calculations concerning money or the number of teachers, and schoolhouses needed. This inquiry has to do with the proper identification and definition of the objectives of education. Can education have its own independent objectives or do these objectives flow from societal definitions of the good life? Is education an autonomous system by itself? Should it harmonize its objectives with those of national development? Is it best to protect and promote the traditional objectives of education in vogue before the birth of the 'developmental era'? Is education a fundamental human right or is it a public utility to service the economy?

The one consistent controversy in this sphere has been between the elitists and the populists in education. The controversy has not been conclusively settled even though there are the pragmatists who believe that it is not a question of 'either/or' but of blending both the objectives judiciously. This, of course, is easier said than done. No concrete, sure-fire formula exists to guarantee the best of both worlds.

QUALITY OF EDUCATION

Discussion of the perfect educational blend tends to focus on the quality of education and its relevance to the immediate demands of living. There is hardly anyone who is against quality. The problem is to protect it while coping with the phenomenal explosion of the social demand for education. Given the large demographic bases, high rates of population growth and the revolution of rising expectations, governments in the developing countries of the world are finding it extremely difficult to cope even with the provision of simple schooling facilities. The dilemma that arises here is between democratization of education on the principle of equality of opportunity and academic/professional selectivity attentive to the quality and composition of required manpower.

RELEVANCE

The other big issue of educational policy is the relevance of education—its contents and methods, standards and duration—to the times. Should education be geared to the needs of today or tomorrow? Since education in itself is a process stretched over a number of years—in different cycles depending upon the kind and level of education—how does one forecast the precise needs of those future years? Manpower projections have only a limited value because of the disparate maturing cycles of different sectors of the economy. Even assuming perfect coordination of policy and its implementation, national perceptions of need would become obsolescent in five years time—given the extraordinary pace of socioeconomic change. Then again, there is the question of the relevance of education to the rural and urban populations, to men and women, to the blacks and whites and to many other differing cultural and ethnic minorities, to the blue-collar technicians and the white-collar professional, to those who go through the formal system of education and those who enter life without a formal educational preparation, to children and to adults, generalists and specialists, and so on. Views range from advocating a single, common national system of education to proposing very exclusive programs of education for each of these categories.

National patterns of secondary education frequently alienate adolescents from their natural moorings while not providing enough saleable skills for the urban labor market. But attempts to rectify this by making it more vocational carry a risk. Education faces a dilemma. If education of rural and tribal children is related to agriculture and forestry, leaders complain that it is a device to keep part of the population perpetually condemned to be hewers of wood and drawers of water. If it is an integrated system of education, it is criticized as unfair to underprivileged children in performance tests because they are supposed to be based and adjudged on concepts and objects outside their own living environment.

BALANCE

If there is one word which sums up the crux of educational policies and planning more than any other, it is balance. The policy-maker and the planner in the field of education are forever required to strike and hold a balance—not a static balance but a dynamic equilibrium—for the simple reason that the constituent variables keep varying. The assumption here is that a balance is almost always possible and acceptable to most since, barring a few dogmatists, people usually do not favor extreme positions. Thus, a national educational system is expected to achieve, in the first instance, a vertical balance between the various stages or levels of education—the elementary, the secondary and the higher, both liberal and technical.

The controversy on the balance between the liberal and the

technical education has held the field for quite some time. Usually the disagreement does not center on whether education should be one or the other but on the methods and techniques of making operational a judicious blend of the two. Should elementary education be planned around the principle of 'learning by doing'—the doing part relating to the economic tasks which have to be performed in the kind of economy prevalent in the immediate environment of the students? Should there be a terminal point at this stage for a good number of students who would discontinue further education anyway? Should there be a bifurcation at the secondary level, one fork providing a terminal point for beginning practice in vocational/technical work and the other fork paving the way for higher academic/professional learning? Should the expansion (a) provide for relative investments in elementary, secondary and higher levels of education, (b) be allowed to 'happen' by the 'natural' flow from one level to the other or should there be a more purposeful regulation, selection, diversion to different streams conforming to some broad picture of the manpower requirements of countries? How should one reconcile individual choice with national need and individual aptitude with the critical shortages in labor? Should technical education, especially at the beginning level of practice, be given through formalized institutions or should it rather be learned on the job or by means of extensive schemes of apprenticeship, paid or unpaid?

Regardless of the precise manner in which planners in different countries have devised answers to this question, one or two broad conclusions seem to be common. First, the educational system is regarded as a pyramid with a broader base and a tapering apex and with certain *inter se* proportions between different levels. Once this is regarded as the logical shape of an educational system distortions can easily be noted and possibly corrected. For instance, a distortion occurs when a system produces a large number of liberally educated but non-employable graduates with critical shortages in skilled occupations existing side by side. The other conclusion concerns the ratios that ought to hold with respect to professionals or specialists and supportive technicians. One UNESCO study suggests normative proportions of 1:5:25, that is one technologist (or comparable specialist) to five middle-level technicians to 25 field-level, semi-skilled functionaries. Instances are not wanting when there has been a superabundance of the higher categories and a paucity of the lower ones. In fact, the chronic shortage of middlelevel skilled manpower has been a prevalent phenomenon in the developing countries. There, again analysis would show the need to maintain a certain balance in education in order to make the whole system viable and produce the required numbers of personnel at different terminal points.

UNORTHODOX APPROACH

Some recent studies (such as the 1974 ILO study on Philippines, popularly called the Ranis Report) have discouraged excessive preoccupation with vocational/technical education at the secondary level. Instead, greater reliance on extensive and imaginative non-formal education to make up for the middle level manpower is recommended. Although the Ranis Report is addressed to the Philippine situation, it makes certain unconventional recommendations which deserve wider notice. For instance, the Ranis Commission notes:[1]

1. We are driven to the conclusion that the optimum policy would be to reduce significantly the growth of enrollment at all levels of the educational system and to divert the resources thereby released to other uses.

2. Schools are not suitable institutions to develop narrowly defined vocational skills; vocational training ought to be mainly provided out of school on the job and other places. What we mean by quality of education is the extent to which schools can encourage children to reason, to digest information and to analyze its implications for action, and of course to read, to write, to reckon and to express themselves. Traditional educationists assert that this is good education and we hold that this is also vocationally useful education. Those who deny this argument must tell us why employers, both private and public, seem to value educated people even when they make no concrete use of their cognitive knowledge.

3. Finally, economic objectives for education are not the whole story. There are important social and political goals which any educational system seeks to satisfy and which may ultimately have economic consequences.

4. We find that too little attention has been given to non-formal education. There is already a widespread network of mass

media which can be used for non-formal education geared to productivity changes; family planning; sanitation and nutrition campaigns; continuing education for the population outside the school system; and so on. To date, the effort has been negligible. We are suggesting the need to consider more fully the social and economic value of non-formal education.

It would seem that education today, whether in the industrialized world or in the developing nations, is on the threshold of new challenges calling for new responses. Yet sometimes one wonders why education which is regarded as a potent influence for innovation and change does not turn its light inwards to bring forth a complete reordering of its values, methods and techniques. Educational planning was supposed to be such a response but unfortunately it seems to be bogged down in models, techniques and equations and has remained largely confined to the coterie of a few planning technocrats. Since an educational system has multiple categories of participants, namely, the policy-makers, the planners, the administrators or managers, teachers, parents and above all, the students—any radical transformation in the system can be brought about only by a consensus among all concerned.

II. PLANNING PROBLEMS

The industrialized nations had to take to educational planning in a serious way because their educational systems were badly disrupted during World War II and they had on hand a heavy backlog of educational needs. It was soon discovered that it was no longer a question of restoring the *status quo ante*; a newer philosophy and technology of education were called for in order to cope with the challenges of the second half of the twentieth century.

According to Phillip H. Coombs,[2] the industrialized nations passed through three educational phases from 1945 to 1970 and now find themselves in a perplexing fourth phase:

1. the Reconstruction Phase;
2. the Manpower Shortage Phase;
3. the Rampant Expansion Phase;
4. the Innovation Phase.

Each phase has yielded its crop of planning problems. The manpower shortage phase is particularly worthy of notice not only because of its impact on the educational planning in Europe but more so because of its side effects on developing nations. It was during this phase that the interest of economists in educational development was aroused rather conspicuously. Education was no longer regarded as 'non-productive sector of the economy which absorbs consumption expenditures,' but rather as an essential 'investment expenditure' for economic growth.

Among the developing nations the need for educational planning was seen in the context of overall national planning—national planning being the chief instrument of modernization and growth. A series of conferences at the ministerial level of government sponsored by UNESCO in the 1960s resulted in quantitative targets being set for education with the ultimate goal of achieving within specified time periods free, compulsory and universal elementary education. The enrollment at the secondary and higher levels of education was projected at rates higher than before. In these exercises, the planning of elementary education was largely based on demographic projections over the next two or three decades. The secondary and the higher levels of education were planned with some very rough and tentative calculations of the major categories of technical manpower, required over four or five plan periods of about five years each. In each instance, educational planning had the characteristics of an arithmetical exercise—trying to match supply and demand where the source of the demand was the hunger for education among millions of first generation learners and the resources needed to satisfy the hunger were finite.

Educational planning during the last quarter of the century has been characterized mainly by three or four approaches.

SOCIAL DEMAND

One of the earliest approaches to planning was based on what is described as social demand for education. This becomes a force in itself and it cannot be easily contained by planning techniques alone. It is a political factor to be reckoned with. In the newly developing countries, more particularly, in many of which modern education has been introduced recently, there is a widespread yearning for education. Regardless of what planners may recognize as the contribution of education to economic development, it is socially regarded as a status ladder, par excellence. Education is looked upon as the key to more lucrative employment, upward social mobility and permanent riddance from menial tasks, especially among first generation learners. They comprise the large masses who were at various stages of serfdom or social disability under the feudal and/or the colonial systems. Since they are also voters, most democratic governments have to cater to their aspirations to the maximum extent possible. Accordingly, planners are expected to assess the social demand for education in the present and in the immediate future, and, to devise plans to meet those demands—stretching in the process the limited resources at hand. One reason why quantity has preempted quality in educational planning is precisely this, namely, a seemingly inexhaustible demand together with extremely inadequate resources. Very often social demand is disguised under manpower-cum-cost benefit jargon nowadays, but by whatever name it is called, it continues to exercise its strength in the planning arena.

HUMAN RESOURCES

Another approach to planning emphasizes the development of human resources. As the term indicates, the concept is that the human element is a resource, a factor, in development. The output efficiency of these factors has naturally to be maximized in order to get the best results in the shortest possible time. In a sense this approach is an extension of the old economic theory which includes labor as one of the four essential prerequisites of production. Just as workers' education and labor welfare are regarded as investments—a way to improve the productivity of labor—so education is regarded as a process of making human resources more diversified and more sophisticated for the task of achieving and sustaining development.

The best known illustration of this approach is the research of Harbison and Myers—both economists specializing in manpower and educational planning.[3] They ranked 57 countries on school enrollments and educational expenditures as indicators of human resource development, and gross national product and percent of farm workers as indicators of economic growth. The countries were divided into four levels of human resource development which was found to correlate positively with economic development. The authors have cautioned that the correlation must not be construed as causal. More analysis of the relationship between educational measures and economic variables is necessary before any conclusion can be asserted. Some planners disregard this caution, however, and dogmatize on the Harbison-Myers findings.

The human resource development approach is different from another phrase which is almost equally popular and is very often used interchangeably, namely, 'investment in man.' The major difference of course is that in the second phase, man is not referred to as a resource. The implication is that although he is the agent of development, he is also the beneficiary and in fact the paramount justification of development. In the human resource development approach, the human factor is subordinated and harnessed to development and is regarded as an inert element whereas in the phrase 'investment in man,' man's conscious motivation is recognized as vital and he is looked upon as the be-all and end-all of development.

MANPOWER DEVELOPMENT

Even more specific to the job market than the concept of human resource development is the manpower approach to educational planning. Here the educational system is viewed as a kind of a subcontractor commissioned to supply certain categories and numbers of skilled workers for the various phases of development. It is job-oriented and is in one sense a swing of the pendulum from the other extreme of *laissez-faire* liberal education. A hangover of the colonial regimes in many newly developing countries resulted in a peculiar phenomenon—the educated unemployed. Graduates well versed in history, the classics, philosophy and the other liberal arts sought work but no one would hire them. Their skills were not saleable. The manpower approach to planning was hailed as a remedy to this situation but its results have hardly justified the claim. There is lacking reliable and comprehensive data on the precise effects of the approach but what evidence exists suggests that by the time the output of the educational system is ready for the market, the labor market has altered and the demand for the product is no longer the same. Despite its limitations, national planning agencies still utilize the manpower approach though generally with a preamble lauding the nobler purposes of education.

COST AND BENEFIT

For purposes of the cost benefit analysis of an investment, it is essential to take into account not only the cash expenditures but also the opportunity cost of a project which implies all real resources used for the project. The opportunity cost is so called because every investment is supposed to represent a choice in favor of a better alternative, thus foregoing either another form of investment or current consumption. The calculation of cost should include not only the actual price of education paid by the student together with the loss of benefits foregone (e.g., salary) but the price and opportunity cost which the community as a whole must bear. As for benefits, these can be calculated by estimating the contribution education will make towards income over the whole working life. The benefits are measured by working out age-earning profiles of two categories of workers, namely, those with a certain level and type of education and those without. The difference in the lifetime earnings of the two average workers can be regarded as the additional income attributable to a better education. The social rates of return are assessed by the increase in national income attributable to the advances in education of its citizenry after deducting the cost of such education to society.

Such a brief description of cost-benefit analysis in education hardly does justice to its mathematical complexity but it does allow a critique of its theoretical and practical implications. The main criticism is that the difference in earnings could also be due to differences in motivation, individual ability, social background, sex, occupation and a whole range of other factors. There is no direct, total and unalterable equation between the type and level of education on the one hand and earnings generated on the other. Likewise, this approach is inclined to ignore the social, cultural and psychological benefits of education. There is, of course, some validity in the cost-benefit approach when deciding the relative rates of return of different projects within the same sector. But the approach does not provide a value-free method of comparing the benefits of projects in different sectors; it cannot offer an objective way of deciding, for instance, whether a hospital is a better investment than a school.

Within limits, cost-benefit studies provide some guidance on the selection of priorities at different levels of education, some clues as to how the cost of education might be regulated, and a heightened awareness of the price a nation must pay if it ignores educational goals.

A new approach is just beginning to develop which involves the application of systems analysis to educational planning. What is being advocated is a broader strategy of human resource development encompassing social, political and cultural ends of national development. According to the systems planners, a comprehensive analysis of the factors associated with modernization and the identification of methods for skill enhancement at various levels in response to the needs of modernization would furnish educational planners with a very effective tool to carry on the task of planning for the future.

NO SUBSTITUTE FOR POLICY

It is obvious that no matter which method or combination of methods is used for educational planning, it will still not answer the policy questions raised earlier. In other words, educational planning like education itself is not a matter merely of technique nor is it subsumed entirely within the context of economic growth. Historically, education precedes economic growth and social change and interacts with them at each successive phase. We cannot afford to dispense with the grand vision of education simply because we need more sophisticated methods to ensure the speedy realization of its objectives. This vision is all the more desirable when the concept of development itself is being thoroughly reappraised. The advanced countries are puzzling over the meaning of development in a post-industrial world while the emerging nations are seeking in development a means of avoiding the pitfalls of industrialization. Both groups are engaged in a search for a new order, a different way of life.

BEYOND DEVELOPMENT

Ralph Miller, writing on the meaning of development and its educational implications, summarizes the quest for a new life in this manner:[4]

It might seem strange if we said our objective was not development, but life. Yet, surely, this is the issue. That the alternative of helping men to live and to have life more abundantly could seem strange only indicates how much we are locked within a particular view. Living more abundantly cannot be measured in the familiar terms of loans and grants and the value of resource transfers from country to country...we have simply got to give up the notion that development is a matter of setting up administrative units to dispense technological solution prescribed by Western, industrial development theory.

According to Miller, the educational implications of the broader conception of development are primarily four.

1. Education must become less formal.
2. Education must be freed from system restrictions and be developed through a variety of specific projects on a similar scale.
3. Education projects must be recognized as experimental and must be monitored so that we may find out what works in specific situations.
4. Education must become more of a service within a complex of development efforts and less of an instructional program for the sake of instruction.

Since the generation that will be in the employment market at the turn of the century has already been born, its education will have to be shaped in accordance with the requirements of the twenty-first century. It will depend upon the kind of society that the policy makers and planners of the world are hoping to build or on the type of society that the futurists expect will emerge by the momentum of forces of change already in motion. In either case, a good deal of futuristic policy-oriented research ard moderniza- tion of the teaching-learning process in educational institutions will be necessary. This will probably call for the extensive use of modern technology in education, not just in terms of audio-visual gadgets imported into the classroom but in the harmonization of the tech- nological aids with systemic changes in education. Very likely the frontiers of education will extend far beyond the classroom and learning will become nonformal. Emphasis on continuing educa- tion comes with the realization that education cannot stop at the end of schooling. It is a life-long process with one goal—the crea- tion of the whole man.

C. DAVID HOLLISTER
JOHN F. JONES

10 Education for Social Development

The supply of manpower qualified for social planning and development is a critical factor in any national development plan. The strategies for manpower training will vary from one country to another, depending on the goals, tasks, and priorities of social development, existing educational facilities, the demand for particular types of personnel, and the country's resources. Thus social development training will encompass a variety of conceptual frameworks and educational models.

This broad approach to education for development permits the role of higher education to be seen in perspective, for it must be remembered that the university is only one institution among many concerned with development. Obviously, in those regions where higher education is in its early stages or where it takes a form quite different to that of an industrialized nation, the educational strategy must adapt to circumstances. Even in those places where higher education is not new, other factors have been taken into account. In many African countries, for instance, professional social work is still embryonic. Although social work training has been given a fairly high priority in many of these nations, it is handicapped by the lack of qualified instructors, the lack of financial resources and indigenous teaching materials, a dearth of adequately prepared students, and the lack of a clear definition of what should be taught.[1] Facing at the same time urgent problems in urban and rural development, their national planners may feel with some justification that the universities cannot be relied upon to meet the extent and diversity of manpower needs. Too many countries have made the mistake of being top heavy in terms of advanced professional education, and in doing so have drained resources necessary for training workers and volunteers at lower levels. Defined manpower policy should include provision for public authorities to join hands with professional associations, schools of social work, and voluntary agencies in formulating national manpower goals and in establishing collaborative training efforts.

Varying Patterns of Social Work Education

Long-term manpower planning is concerned with the maximum utilization of resources, and in this context institutions of higher learning play a vital role. In most countries professional education in schools of social work is the preferred means of training personnel for a broad range of leadership functions in social welfare and development. Professional education usually emphasizes the knowledge and skill required for community-based efforts, as well as for national policy and planning. There is no single pattern of sponsorship of schools of social work. Some are attached to universities; others are affiliated with technical institutions. Funding may come from public or private sources, though there is a trend in many parts of the world to rely heavily on government financing.

The length of professional education varies from one to five years, depending on the higher education patterns in different areas and the previous qualifications of applicants to professional schools. It is not uncommon for schools affiliated to universities to offer graduate education, while schools not attached to universities may see the provision of education at the undergraduate level as their principal function. To generalize about the length and format of professional education is, however, difficult because of the differing status of social work in different regions and changing patterns of education.

While there is obviously room for international cooperation in manpower training, those countries which have previously sent their social workers abroad for graduate education are doing so now with less eagerness. Part of the reluctance is of course financial, but there are deeper reasons. As Dame Eileen Younghusband has pointed out, a school of social work may induce in its students acute conflict if it successfully prepares them for a level of practice far removed from that of existing social agencies and the values of a particular culture.[2] This note of caution applies to all students and their teachers, but it has special relevance for overseas students; the effects of foreign education are often perceived as less than desirable by sponsors at home. Besides, many countries prefer to begin their manpower development programs at the top, by establishing training opportunities for social welfare personnel at leadership levels, and the establishment of an indigenous professional school is undoubtedly the most efficient and effective way to do this. In Sierra Leone, for example, trained personnel are so scarce that the government is reluctant to let its top-level workers go abroad for study even though scholarships and fellowships are available for this purpose. The trend to establish indigenous educational resources can be expected to change further the content and form of professional education for social development.

SOCIAL WORK EDUCATION AND SOCIAL DEVELOPMENT

To propose a single model for manpower training would be to neglect the cultural differences that exist within and between geographic regions and to ignore the variations prevalent in educational institutions throughout the world. Similarly, it would be a mistake to tie social development to a single academic discipline (such as social work) as it would to confine its study to present, largely arbitrary, classifications within academia, such as the baccalaureate or Master's degree. Fred Riggs, in his study of administration in developing countries, has drawn attention to the ecology of development. Management influences and is influenced by the prevailing culture; culture in turn relates to the educational system; and education itself depends on the economy.[3] Each set of administrative techniques is possible only if supported by a complex of other structures. As a consequence, developmental administration must be studied in the context of anthropology, sociology, economics, political science and so on. If this is true of developmental administration, it is true of social development itself. Hopefully, a number of academic disciplines will come in time to concentrate on the problems of development. Meanwhile, it is entirely reasonable for any one discipline to make social development its object of study, provided the staking out of territory does not suggest a right of eminent domain.

There is an emerging concern on the part of social workers with social development. The aims of social work and those of social development match,[4] and if social work methods seem at times to fail the demands of development, it is due in part to the expanse of territory social work has been called upon to cover. The activities of social workers are sometimes clinical in nature, sometimes directed towards helping the healthy enhancement of social functioning, and sometimes related to policy and planning.[5] There is no reason whatever why social work should cease activity in any of these areas, since such services are necessary in all communities. No contradiction exists between direct services and social policy, in and of themselves, and schools of social work have generally made that assumption in drawing up their curricula. Nonetheless, without a clear focus on social development (however expressed), social work practice and education run the risk of a scattergun approach to the problems of society.

It was from this perspective that the International Conference of Ministers Responsible for Social Welfare, which met in New York in 1968, laid particular stress on the 'developmental and preventive' functions of social welfare. This priority, according to the Ministers, represents a major shift in social welfare policy and 'would require a marked re-orientation of existing resources, programs and personnel.'[6] Later on, the First Asian Conference of Ministers Responsible for Social Welfare declared that curricula on social work training should be geared to social developmental goals and constantly examined, reviewed and evaluated in the light of changing needs. 'Social work education should provide trained and qualified social workers with a broader knowledge in working with related professions in the social services and should equip them with the relationships and communication skills required to facilitate the implementation of an interdisciplinary approach to social development.'[7]

The rationale underlying this recommendation lay in the role of social workers as perceived by the participants of the First Asian Conference:

1. promoting social policy and planning in development;
2. ensuring social justice with particular reference to more equitable distribution of the national wealth;
3. encouraging participation by the people in policy formulation, planning, and implementation;

4. improving the social and cultural infrastructure by institution building.

The significance of this role definition is apparent in the terminology of 'participation of the people,' 'institution building', 'social justice' and 'social policy and planning.' Such thinking puts social work concerns firmly in the area of political and economic events.

OBSERVATIONS ON CURRICULUM CONTENT

Incorporation of the concept of social development into social work education can best be achieved through a coherent and systematic curriculum. A model for such a curriculum is offered below, but, before attempting its outline, a word of caution is appropriate. It is not feasible to design a program which enables each student to master the full array of social development skills. The complexity of the development process, limited faculty resources and time constraints rule out so ambitious a goal. Moreover, the nature of social development itself demands cooperative community interaction wherein a team approach, combining the expertise of a variety of professions and disciplines, is utilized. Each curriculum is, therefore, a compromise. Its aim is to enable students to master a specific group of social development skills in keeping with the student's own interests and abilities, and at the same time to convey a conceptual understanding of a broader range of social development skills and their interrelationship so that the graduate becomes adept at working within a group to achieve the aims of social development.

The compromise to be achieved in the curriculum will also depend upon internal factors such as the expertise of the faculty, the traditions and mission of the educational institution and on external factors relating to financial support, teaching material available and cooperative arrangements. For instance, in the model we propose there is no provision for teaching clinical skills, though many schools of social work give such instruction high priority.

In November 1972, a regional conference sponsored by the United Nations was held in Bangkok to consider the problems and prospects of schools of social work contributing to development in Asia, and to design a long-term action framework to help schools address themselves to developmental issues.[8] The findings and conclusions of the conference have significance not only for Asian schools but for schools elsewhere concerned with development. Because of their applicability to social work education in general, the observations of the participants can be used to formulate assumptions regarding curriculum content. The principal assumptions relevant to curriculum content may be summarized as follows:

1. Social work students should possess a broad knowledge base in the social sciences, including economics, sociology and political science.

2. Social development calls for an interdisciplinary approach. Certain social problems (mass poverty, over-population, maldistribution of wealth, illiteracy and the like) should receive explicit interdisciplinary attention in the curriculum.

3. Social workers need to be more skillful in political situations and more aggressive in advocacy, and the educational process in schools should reflect this goal in the knowledge and skills components of the curriculum. Such education should be of a liberating, not domesticating, kind—an education which develops critical consciousness, social awareness and personal responsibility.

4. Nonviolent social change should be the preferred social change strategy.

5. Social work students should not only draw from other disciplines in acquiring a social development focus, but they should also master the skills necessary to work with other disciplines. This team approach can be seen as an intersubcultural relationship, each discipline possessing its own subculture.

6. Social workers play an important role in local community development. Education, therefore, should attend to the organizational aspects of developing local communities and local leadership, as well as to stimulating popular participation.

7. In their eagerness for broad social change, social workers should not neglect their traditional concern for people who are bypassed by existing social services. Getting people into the mainstream of society and helping them become contributing members is a distinctively social work developmental concern, and this should be a specific focus in the curriculum.

8. The respective roles of government, voluntary organizations and the private sector in social services should be studied. The investigation may not lead to espousing one form of service

delivery, but it should suggest a variety of methods in which services can be provided and adapted to the needs of a particular population.

9. National and regional government policy should be examined critically in the light of social priorities. This requires, first, knowledge about the political process of establishing priorities and, secondly, the effort to determine what are just and feasible social goals. National budgets need to be examined to see how much priority is given to social welfare in contrast, for example, to defense.

10. The prevailing milieu of social work education varies from country to country. The recognition of this fact should promote tolerance of different patterns and content of education.

The Social Development Concept in American Social Work Education

While many of the above assumptions have for some time guided facets of American social work education, the concept of social development has only recently been made an explicit focus in the United States. Likewise, most of the component skills of social development have been present in American social work and its professional curricula under the unifying concept of social welfare, but not until recently have they been organized into a developmental perspective. A recent bulletin of the school of Social Service Administration at the University of Chicago illustrates this point in describing a newly developed Master's level concentration in social development:

The Social Development program is designed to examine large scale social welfare problems and the institutions that have been established to deal with these problems.

This program is a reflection of the growing concern on the part of the social work profession with strategies for intervention in the complex network of social organizations and systems. Historically, a series of approaches have emerged as vehicles for intervention: policy, planning, administration, and community organization. These approaches have frequently pulled in different directions, and an emphasis on the differences among them has frequently obscured commonalities.[9]

In the last few years a number of schools of social work in the United States have established curricula in social development, and more seem likely to do so. Most of these programs are at the Master's level, but at least two schools of social work have developed a doctoral program focussed on social development,[10] and another has both master's and bachelor's programs in social development.[11] Examination of the bulletins and curriculum materials of these schools reveals a good deal of consensus on the component skills of social development, in that community organization, policy development, planning, research and evaluation, and administration are typically identified as key components.[12]

A GENERAL MODEL FOR SOCIAL DEVELOPMENT

A curriculum for social development training should be derived from a model or set of assumptions regarding the aims and processes of social development. There can, of course, be many models of social development. The model presented here represents just one conceptualization.

Social development may be defined as the process of planned institutional change to bring about a better fit between human needs and social policies and programs. The use of the phrase 'planned institutional change' points out two things: first, social development requires deliberate social intervention; second, the focus is primarily on changing social institutions—policies, agencies, programs, and social roles and expectations, and not primarily on changing individuals, though some institutional changes do require corresponding changes in the collective attitudes and expectations of a population.

The phrase 'better fit' in the definition implies that some set of values will be used to estimate whether the changes contemplated would indeed provide a better fit or correspondence. The humanitarian and democratic values traditionally held in social work provide a basis for making these judgments, though these values will not resolve all the issues and dilemmas raised by the prospect of social development.

Social development emphasizes both the need for more comprehensive and coordinated policy and planning on a local, regional and national basis, and the need to help indigenous groups to organize so as to influence political and bureaucratic structures to more completely address their particular needs. Social development thus stresses the need for reciprocal influence between the community and social policy at all stages in the development of social programs. The diagram shown in the Flow Chart illustrates the process.

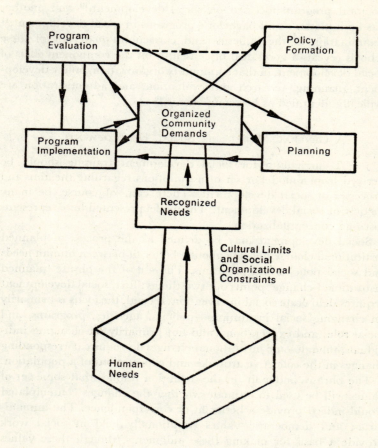

This is a general scheme of social development. We start with human needs. The base of the diagram represents the total range of human needs—nutrition, shelter, protection and so on—all needs, known and unknown. In any society, however, only some of these needs are recognized. Culture shapes the definition of needs. Some needs will be cultivated, nurtured, and valued. Some are only rather grudgingly recognized, tolerated, and starved along, for example, sexual fulfillment in a production oriented society. Still others are suppressed. No society fills all needs completely. Culture—including language itself—sets limits on which needs are recognized. The 'trunk' of the diagram represents the limits set by culture and social organization.

The first box above the base of human needs represents this selective recognition and awareness of certain needs. The initial recognition of new needs probably comes more often from artists, novelists, humanists and clinicians than from social and behavioral scientists, though the latter pick up the idea and help disseminate it. Initially only a few are aware. Later the awareness may spread, but the rate of spread is affected by the extent to which the new idea is *consistent* with the culture and social organization. Conceptualizations of human needs that challenge the existing culture and social organization have a slower diffusion rate.

The second box above the base of human need represents the extent to which awareness of needs becomes organized into collective demand within the community for organized response to needs. Awareness does not automatically galvanize people into organization for action, however. The social organization of a particular society or of a community channels and constrains the amount and the content of communication.

Societies with a fatalistic philosophy, an elitist political organization and a tradition of *noblesse oblige* will be slower to organize for collective expression around new concepts of need than will societies with a pragmatic philosophy, a participatory political organization, and a tradition of self-help. One important role in the social development process is that of the community organizer who helps people to identify their needs and to organize for the collective expression of them.[13]

As needs are organized into demands the potential for political influence grows. In the model presented here this influence directly affects not only policy formulation; it also directly affects planning, program implementation, administration, and even evaluation (recall the sizable portion of the literature on program evaluation which is given over to political considerations as opposed to strictly technical discussion of the conduct of evaluation).[14]

We are not glibly assuming that the mere organization and expression of demands by a group automatically induces the desired policy outputs, plans, and programs. Obviously this does not happen. We are drawing on one of Thomas Dye's models of policy production—that which Dye calls the 'group equilibrium' model:

> Public policy at any given time is the equilibrium reached in the group struggle. This equilibrium is determined by the relative influence of any interest groups. Changes in the relative influence of any interest groups can be expected to result in changes in public policy; policy will move in the direction desired by the groups gaining in influence, and away from the desires of groups losing influence.
>
> . . . the influence of groups is determined by their numbers, wealth, organizational strength, leadership, access to decision makers, and internal cohesion.[15]

There are, of course, competing explanations of how public policy is formulated—elitism, rationalism, and incrementalism have also been suggested as models of policy formulation. We would argue, however, that (a) the group equilibrium model provides the closest fit for American society, and (b) even if other models occasionally come into play, this only implies a change in social strategy, not a weakening of the general model for social development we propose here.

Turning again to the Flow Chart, note the direct influence of program evaluation on program administration and on planning. Feedback from evaluation studies in this country occasionally influences policy, but probably much less often than commonly supposed.[16] Political influences, rather than knowledge of program effectiveness, predominate in policy formulation. But program evaluation does also directly feedback into the implementation of specific programs and into planning processes.

In this general scheme of social development each box contains activities at several levels. For example, social policy formulation in this country occurs at national, state, regional and local levels. Planning may be comprehensive planning focussed on a geographic area or it may be directed at certain categories of events or people that cut across geographic boundaries, for example, planning services to the developmentally disabled.

Program implementation can occur at many levels, which usually in this country correspond to political jurisdictions, e.g., federal, state, regional, county, municipal, and so on.

Likewise program evaluation may range from the examination of broad, comprehensive programs at the federal level down to examination of minute variations of very small programs.

This model, like all models, is an oversimplification of reality. Other connections could be made within it. For example, planning processes to some extent react upon policy formulation and constrain it in some ways. Likewise, experience with program implementation—the actual administration of a program—also reacts upon planning and sets some limits on planning processes. But rather than clutter the model with all possible connections, we have attempted to draw out the main lines of influence.

The advantages of this model of social development may be summarized briefly, as follows:

First, the model points up the need for social programs to be rooted in social policy affording a more comprehensive, less piecemeal approach to servicing human needs.

Second, it calls attention to the limitations—cultural blinders—on our perception and conceptualization, into which we are typically socialized as part of growing up and living in a particular culture. If we are aware these barriers exist, we may be somewhat better prepared to break through them.

Third, the model makes the identification of human needs problematic, not assumed. At the same time, it leaves open new conceptualizations of human needs, in that it does not assume any particular list of needs.

Fourth, it realistically places social intervention in its political context. Certainly the upper portion, and ultimately all of the linkages can be seen as political processes, at least in part.

Fifth, it stresses the importance of reciprocal influences of policy formulation and community demands on each other.

Sixth, it points out that social development involves many processes occurring simultaneously. Simultaneous action on several levels may be necessary to effect change. Conversely, one may initiate the process of social development at many points, not just one point.

Seventh, it identifies a set of core skills for social development—community organization, policy formulation and analysis, planning, administration, and program evaluation. It thus can be used as a curriculum guide for education in social development.

ORGANIZING A CURRICULUM FOR SOCIAL DEVELOPMENT

Relying on the foregoing model, it is comparatively easy to establish the objectives and content of a curriculum stressing social development. The developmental emphasis requires that the educational program focus simultaneously on human needs, social policy, the political and economic context of action, community organization, social planning, administration and research. Each of these foci implies specific curriculum dimensions.[17]

1. *The Identification of Human Needs.* The curriculum should provide an opportunity to identify and examine basic human needs, such as nutrition, housing, health, education, and so on. While it may not be possible to achieve consensus as to what constitutes the full range of 'basic' needs, the curriculum should at least raise issues as to which needs are fundamental, and the extent to which, in a given society, these needs are not presently met.

2. *Social Policy.* In view of human needs, what are just and feasible social goals? How can alternative policy proposals be evaluated? The curriculum should provide: (a) a value system in keeping with the 'common good', which involves a humanistic approach toward social development; (b) an understanding of the substantive areas of social policy; (c) an ability to analyze, compare, and formulate alternative policy proposals; (d) an understanding of and preference for the development of comprehensive and systemic social policies versus *ad hoc*, remedial, and 'patch-up' policies.

3. *The Political and Economic Context of Action.* The curriculum should address the political and economic feasibility of policy and program proposals. This implies in turn, an examination of processes of economic development and of political structures and values in the society, with consideration of strategies of alternative economic development and of political advocacy and action.

4. *Community Organization.* The curriculum should present content on the social organization of the society and its institutions, with particular attention to the implications for community organizing and development. The objective is to develop students' abilities to work simultaneously with indigenous community groups and with bureaucratic systems, so as to help strengthen indigenous leadership to identify needs and effective strategies for collective self-help.

5. *Social Planning.* The curriculum should present both theories

and techniques for planning the establishment and modification of social service programs. Stress should be placed on the need for grounding planning in social policy, and on the reciprocal influences on planning of political, economic and social structures and processes.

6. *Administration.* Theories and techniques of organization and management should be presented in the curriculum, with particular emphasis on administrative models that induce organizational responsiveness to individual needs, and which build in evaluation and feedback.

7. *Research.* Two separate but related purposes compel the inclusion of research design and techniques in the curriculum.[18] The first is the utility of research skills in the planning process. The assessment of needs and of present capacities to meet needs both require skills in descriptive research, including quantitative skills in data collection and analysis. The second is the need for evaluation of social programs. The curriculum should include content on the appropriate use of various research designs and on the problems of utilization of findings.

Two additional, more general objectives for the curriculum can also be identified:

1. the imparting of a scientific and scholarly orientation towards the advancement of social work professional knowledge and social development;
2. the cultivation of an interdisciplinary approach to social development, and the promotion of interdisciplinary relationships in the educational institution.[19]

With the possible exception of the first and third dimensions all of the above dimensions should be viewed as having both knowledge and skill components. In this way one may hope to avoid the dichotomy that has arisen in some schools of social work between 'theory' and 'methods' or between 'theory' and 'practice'. An example of this integration may be found in a course on human service program evaluation which on the one hand explicates formal designs for program evaluation and the administrative, ethical and political factors in evaluation, but which on the other hand requires each student to actually undertake the design of an evaluation for a real, ongoing human service program or agency.

In many ways, social development requires a generalist: one who can move quite quickly back and forth, in and among needs identification, community organization, policy formulation, planning, administration and so on; one who is familiar and skilled in most aspects of the process; one who in a sense can work both the bureaucratic policy making and the community advocacy sides of the street.

CONCLUSION

As the concepts of social development gain wider acceptance throughout the world,[20] the demand for qualified social development workers will increase. This will occur as governmental and private human service agencies recognize their needs for planning and program evaluation, as more and more consumer and client groups desire to get themselves organized, as planning at the regional level comes more into vogue, and as governmental agencies attempt to develop more comprehensive social policy and more coordinated and integrated human service systems.

The need for social development workers will generate new programs geared specifically toward education for social development. These will be organized in various formats under differing auspices, but the curriculum of such programs will typically include emphases on human needs, social policy, planning, community organization and development, administration, research techniques, and the political, social, and economic contexts of action.

Notes

Chapter I
INTRODUCTION TO DEVELOPMENT: AN INTERNATIONAL PERSPECTIVE

1. United Nations, 'The Role of Social Factors in Development,' Background Paper, No. 2, p. 2. Expert Group Meeting on Social Policy and Planning, Stockholm, 1969.
2. Ira Sharkansky argues this point precisely in his *The United States: A Study of a Developing Country* (New York: David McKay, 1975).
3. Donella H. Meadows, *et al.*, *The Limits to Growth* (New York: Universe Books, 1972) p. 23. See also Dennis L. Meadows and Donella H. Meadows, *Toward Global Equilibrium: Collected Papers* (Cambridge, Mass.: Wright-Allen, 1973). A more optimistic appraisal of the global situation is presented in Ervin Laslo (ed.), *The World System* (New York: George Braziller, 1973). While the contributors to *The World System* advocate caution in the interpretation of *The Limits to Growth,* they offer few facts that would contradict the conclusions of the Club of Rome.
4. *Fourth National Development Plan, 1968–72.* Plan Organization, Tehran, 1968, p. 39.
5. *Third Five Year Plan, 1965–70.* Planning Commission, Government of Pakistan, 1965, p. 40.
6. *Perspectives of Social Development in the ECAFE Region in the Second Development Decade,* prepared by the Economic Commission for Asia and the Far East, Social Development Division, Bangkok, 1970.
7. United Nations, *Compendium of Housing Statistics,* 1972–74.
8. Frances Moore Lappé and Joseph Collins, *Food First: Beyond the Myth of Scarcity* (Boston: Houghton Mifflin, 1977).
9. Susan George, *How the Other Half Dies* (Montclair, N. J.: Allanheld, Osmun, 1977).
10. Alden Whitman, 'Food, but not for the Poor and Hungry,' *Chronicle of Higher Education,* Vol. XV, No. 4 (September 26, 1977), p. 15.
11. Harold Wilensky and Charles N. Lebeaux, *Industrial Society and Social Welfare* (New York: Russell Sage Foundation, 1958), p. 17.
12. P. D. Kulkarni, 'The Developmental Function and Interdisciplinary Nature of Social Welfare,' *Education for Social Change,* Proceedings of the XVIIth

International Conference on Social Welfare, Nairobi, July 6-9, 1974. (New York: International Council on Social Welfare, 1975), pp. 24-33.

13. C. Inayatullah, 'Political Context of Programs of Rural Development and Rural Poverty' in Arnold Wehmhoerner (ed.), *Effective Anti-Poverty Strategies* (Bangkok: Friedrich-Ebert-Stiftung, 1974), pp. 114-26.

14. Gunnar Myrdal, *The Challenge of World Poverty* (New York: Vintage Books, 1970), pp. 97-138.

15. For further discussion on agricultural technology and social policy, see V. K. R. V. Rao, *Growth with Justice in Asian Agriculture* (Geneva: United Nations Research Institute for Social Development, 1974).

16. C. Inayatullah, *Cooperatives and Development in Asia* (Geneva: United Nations Research Institute for Social Development, 1972). See also *Rural Cooperatives as Agents of Change: A Research Report and a Debate*, Vol. 8 (Geneva: United Nations Research Institute for Social Development, 1975).

17. Inayatullah, 'Political Context of Programs . . .,' p. 121.

18. Robert L. Heilbroner, *An Inquiry into the Human Prospect* (New York: W. W. Norton, 1974), p. 136.

19. The need in a federal form of government, such as the United States, for coordination between levels of administration is extensively studied in *Regional Decision Making: New Strategies for Substate Districts*, A Report of the Advisory Commission on Intergovernmental Relations, Washington, D. C., October 1973.

20. P. D. Kulkarni, 'Planning for Balanced Social and Economic Development in India' in *Planning for Balanced Social and Economic Development: Six Country Case Studies* (New York: United Nations, 1964), pp. 12-13.

21. Erwin Kristoffersen, 'The Inter-Relation of Social and Economic Development' in Kristoffersen (ed.), *One World Only* (Bangkok: Friedrich-Ebert-Stiftung, 1971), p. 7.

22. *Research Notes*, No. 4, United Nations Institute for Social Development, Geneva, 1974.

23. D. V. McGranahan, *et al.*, *Contents and Measurement of Socioeconomic Development* (New York: Praeger, 1972).

24. Wolf Scott, Helen Argalias and D. V. McGranahan, *The Measurement of Real Progress at the Local Level* (Geneva: United Nations Research Institute for Social Development, 1973), pp. 56-61.

25. Daniel P. Moynihan, *The Politics of a Guaranteed Income* (New York: Random House, 1973).

Chapter II

A Unified Approach to Development

1. 'In the last half-century, the state, in all the rich countries of the Western world, has become a democratic "Welfare State", with fairly explicit commitments to the broad goals of economic development, full employment, equality of opportunity for the young, social security, and protected minimum standards as regards not only of income, but nutrition, housing, health and education, for people of all regions and social groups. The Welfare State is nowhere, as yet, an accomplishment; it is continually in the process of coming into being.'

Gunnar Myrdal, *Beyond the Welfare State* (London: Gerald Duckworth, 1960), p. 45.

2. The discussion here draws in part on Chapter XIV, 'Conditions of Growth and Development' in the writer's study, *India's Development Experience* (New York: St. Martin's Press, 1975), pp. 387-414.

3. 'There are too many different ways in which a state can pursue the end of social welfare, and too many possible combinations of all the methods which might be adopted for this purpose. And there is no scientific procedure by which to determine what, in an ideal Welfare State, would be the relation between government action on the one hand and individual liberty on the other.' T. H. Marshall, *Class, Citizenship and Social Development* (New York: Anchor Books, Doubleday & Company, 1965), p. 281.

Chapter III
STRATEGIES FOR SOCIAL DEVELOPMENT:
AN ANALYTICAL APPROACH

1. United Nations, Commission for Social Development, *Report on a Unified Approach to Development Analysis and Planning: Report of the Secretary General* (E/CN. 5/490, 1973), p. 2.

2. United Nations, Commission for Social Development, *Report on a Unified Approach to Development Analysis and Planning: Preliminary Report of the Secretary General* (E/CN. 5/477, 1972), pp. 12-19.

3. Ibid., p. 20.

4. P. J. Pajestka, *Social Dimensions of Development* (New York: United Nations, 1970), p. 14.

5. Martin Rein, *Social Policy: Issues of Choice and Change* (New York: Random House, 1970), p. 181.

6. Oscar Morgenstern, 'Game Theory: Theoretical Aspects' in David L. Sills (ed.), *International Encyclopedia of the Social Sciences* (New York: Macmillan, 1968), Vol. VI, pp. 62-9.

7. Fred M. Cox, *et al.*, (eds.), *Strategies of Community Organization* (Itasca: Peacock, 1974), pp. 161-73.

8. F. W. Riggs, *Administration in Developing Countries: The Theory of Prismatic Society* (Boston: Houghton-Mifflin, 1964), pp. 413-18.

9. United Nations, *Report on a Unified Approach . . .*, 1973, pp. 8-10.

10. J. A. Ponsioen, *Social Welfare Policy* (The Hague: Mouton, 1962), pp. 37-8.

11. R. M. Titmus, *Commitment to Welfare* (New York: Pantheon Books, 1968), pp. 130-31.

12. United Nations, *Social Policy and Planning in National Development: Report of the Meeting of Experts on Social Policy and Planning*, Stockholm, 1969. (E/CN. 5/455, 1969).

13. United Nations, *Report on a Unified Approach . . .*, 1972, p. 24

14. United Nations, Economic Commission for Latin America, *Social Change and Social Development Policy in Latin America*, 1970, pp. 279-80.

15. R. M. Titmus, *Developing Social Policy in Conditions of Rapid Social Change: The Role of Social Welfare, Proceedings of the XVIth International Conference on*

Social Welfare, The Hague, 1972. (New York: International Council on Social Welfare, 1972), pp. 40-1.

16. United Nations, Commission for Social Development, *Popular Participation and its Practical Implications for Development: Note by the Secretary General*, (E/CN. 5/496, 1974), pp. 4-5.

17. United Nations, *Social Change and Social Development Policy in Latin America*, p. 297.

18. Ibid., pp. 299-300.

19. United Nations, Economic Commission for Asia and the Far East, *Social Development in Asia—Retrospect and Prospect* (New York: United Nations, 1971), p. 53.

20. United Nations, *Social Change and Social Development Policy in Latin America*, pp. 196-7.

21. Jan Tinbergen, *Development Planning* (New York: McGraw-Hill, 1967), p. 117.

22. Kenneth E. Boulding, 'The Boundaries of Social Policy,' *Soical Work*, Vol. XII, No. 1 (January 1967), pp. 3-11.

23. United Nations, Commission for Social Development, *Report on Unified Approach to Development Analysis and Planning: Note by the Secretary General* (E/CN. 5/519, 1974), pp. 32-3.

24. Ibid., pp. 25-8.

25. For further discussion on development poles and development centers, see Tormod Hermansel, 'Development Poles and Development Centers in National and Regional Development: Elements of a Theoretical Framework' in A. R. Kulkinsi (ed.), *Growth Poles and Growth Centers in Regional Planning* (The Hague; Mouton, 1972), Ch. I.

26. For further discussion on aggregation and disaggregation, see G. A. Almond and James S. Coleman (eds.), *The Politics of the Developing Areas* (Princeton University Press, 1960).

27. A. Waterston, *Development Planning: Lessons of Experience* (Baltimore: John Hopkins Press, 1965), p. 167.

28. United Nations, *Report on a Unified Approach . . .*, 1972, p. 49.

Chapter IV
INTERNATIONAL COOPERATION FOR DEVELOPMENT

1. *Partners in Development: Report of the Commission on International Development* (New York: Praeger, 1970), p. 4.

2. Walter A. Friedlander, *International Social Welfare* (Englewood Cliffs: Prentice-Hall, 1975), p. 54.

3. Everett Kleinjans, *Communication and Change in Developing Countries* (Honolulu: East-West Center, 1975), p. 6.

4. Gunnar Myrdal, *The Challenge of World Poverty* (New York: Panthean, 1970), p. 371.

5. Daniel S. Sanders, 'The Role of Social Welfare—An Integrated Approach to Development,' *Development and Participation: Operational Implications for Social Welfare*, Proceedings of the XVIIth International Conference on Social Welfare, Nairobi, July 6-9, 1974. (New York: International Council on Social Welfare, 1975), pp. 131-2.

6. Katherine A. Kendall, 'Focus on Prevention and Development: New Approaches to Social Work Education,' *A Developmental Outlook for Social Work Education* (New York: International Association of Schools of Social Work, 1974), pp. 24-5.

7. United Nations, *Development in the 1980s: Approach to A New Strategy*, New York, 1978.

8. *Partners in Development*, pp. 14-22.

9. Myrdal, pp. 346-7.

10. Friedlander, pp. 29-31.

11. *Partners in Development*, p. 4.

12. Ibid., p. 130.

13. Over the past fifteen years, nonmilitary assistance to developing countries from the 'First World' has totalled approximately $57 billion, with concessional loans comprising an additional $84 billion. In the 1960s the United States contributed more than half of that assistance, and in recent years it has contributed nearly a third of the aid, private investment and technical assistance that has flowed from the wealthy, industrialized nations to the underdeveloped world.

14. *Partners in Development*, p. 28.

15. *Toward Accelerated Development: Proposals for the Second United Nations Development Decade* (New York: United Nations, 1970), p. 5.

16. *Proceedings of the International Conference of Ministers Responsible for Social Welfare* (New York: United Nations, 1969).

17. James W. Howe, *The U.S. and the Developing World: Agenda for Action 1974* (New York: Praeger, 1974).

18. Myrdal, p. 365.

19. Ismail Satsry Abdullah quoted in *Time* (December 22, 1975), p. 42.

Chapter V

SOCIAL POLICIES AND SOCIAL DEVELOPMENT:
A HUMANISTIC-EGALITARIAN PERSPECTIVE

1. For a comprehensive discussion of social policy, see David G. Gil, *Unravelling Social Policy* (Cambridge, Mass.: Schenkman, 1973); Peter L. Berger and Thomas Luckman, *The Social Construction of Reality* (New York: Doubleday, 1966).

2. George A. Theodorson and Achilles G. Theodorson, *A Modern Dictionary of Sociology* (New York: Thomas Y. Crowell, 1969).

3. Erich Fromm, *Man For Himself* (New York, Toronto: Rinehart, 1947).

Chapter VI

PROGRAM PLANNING

1. Bert F. Hoselitz (ed.), *Social Development Symposium* (Paris: United Nations Scientific, Educational and Cultural Organization, 1965), p. 29.
T. H. Marshall, 'Welfare in the Context of Social Development,' in John S. Morgan (ed.), *Welfare and Wisdom* (Toronto: University of Toronto Press, 1965).

John Romanyshyn, *Social Welfare: From Charity to Justice* (New York: Random House, 1971), pp. 375-406.

United Nations, *International Social Development Review*, 2 (1971), pp. 3-17.

United Nations, *Report of the Working Party on Social Development and Report of the Expert Group on Social Development* (Economic Commission for Asia and The Far East, New York, 1971) p. 575.

2. Eugen Pusic, 'Levels of Social and Economic Development as Limits to Welfare Policy,' *Social Service Review*, 45 (December, 1971), pp. 400-13.

3. Melvin G. Blase, *Institution Building: A Source Book* (Agency for International Development, U.S. Department of State, 1973), pp. 4-8.

4. United Nations, *Report of the Working Party*, op. cit.

5. David G. Gil, *Unravelling Social Policy* (New Jersey: Schenkman, 1973), pp. 11-56.

T. H. Marshall, 'Welfare in the Context of Social Development', op. cit.

John Romanyshyn, *Social Welfare: From Charity to Justice*, op. cit.

6. N. Gilbert and H. Specht, *Dimensions of Social Welfare Policy* (New Jersey: Prentice-Hall, 1974), pp. 25-53.

7. Gil, *Unravelling Social Policy*, op. cit.

8. United Nations, *Social Change and Social Development Policy in Latin America* (New York: United Nations, 1970) pp. 169-85.

9. Blase, *Institution-Building: A Source Book*, op. cit.

Chapter VII
Institution Building

1. United Nations, Department of Economic and Social Affairs, 1974 *Report on the World Social Situation* (New York: United Nations, 1975), p. 6.

2. Lester B. Pearson, *Partners in Development* (New York: Praeger, 1969), pp. 29-39.

3. United Nations, *1974 Report on the World Social Situation*, p. 226.

4. 'Education,' World Bank, Sector Working Paper, Washington, D. C., 1971, pp. 6-7.

5. W. W. Rostow, *Politics and the Stages of Growth* (London: Cambrdige University Press, 1971), p. 5.

6. V. K. R. V. Rao, *Growth with Justice in Asian Agriculture* (Geneva: United Nations Research Institute for Social Development, 1974), pp. 1-3.

7. Uinberg Chai, *Moderning Process of a Developing Nation* (Pacific Palisades: Goodyear Publishing Co., 1972), p. 15.

8. Salima Omer, *Institution Building and Comprehensive Social Development* (Doct. Diss., Brandeis University, 1975), p. 135.

9. John Kenneth Galbraith, *A China Passage* (Boston: Houghton Mifflin, 1973), pp. 106-7.

10. Jan Myrdal and Gun Kessle, *China: The Revolution Continued* (New York: Pantheon Books, 1970), p. 53.

11. Committee of Concerned Asian Scholars, *China: Inside the People's Republic* (New York: Bantam Books, 1972), pp. 150-66.

12. Dan Leon, *The Kibbutz: A New Way of Life* (Oxford: Pergamon, 1969), p. 48.

13. Terance E. Cook and Patrick M. Morgan, *Participatory Democracy* (San Francisco: Canfield, 1974), p. 4.
14. Raymond S. Franklin and William K. Tabb, 'The Challenge of Radical Political Economics,' *Journal of Economic Issues*, Vol. VIII, No. 1 (March 1974), pp. 127-50.

Chapter VIII
STRATEGIES OF CITIZEN PARTICIPATION

1. General Assembly Resolution 2542 (XXIV), Article 5.
2. United Nations, *International Development Strategy:* Action Programme of the General Assembly of the Second United Nations Development Decade, New York, 1970.
3. Gabriel A. Almond and Sidney Verba, *The Civic Culture: Political Attitudes and Democracy in Five Nations* (Princeton, N. J.: Princeton University Press, 1963) p. 5.
4. *Preliminary Report on a Unified Approach to Development Analysis in Planning*, p. 36.
5. F. Paulo Friere, *Pedagogy of the Oppressed* (New York: Seabury, 1974), p. 40.
6. Charles J. Grosser, *New Directions in Community Organization: From Enabling to Advocacy* (New York: Praeger, 1963), p. 25.
7. Jon Van Til and Sally Van Til, 'Citizen Participation in Social Policy: The End of the Cycle,' *Social Problems*, Vol. XVII, No. 3 (Winter 1970), p. 322.
8. Roland Warren, Stephen M. Rose, and Ann F. Berginder, *The Structure of Urban Reform* (Lexington, Mass.: Lexington Books, 1974), p. 119.
9. Loretta Nizzi Benz, 'Citizen Participation Reconsidered,' *Social Work*, Vol. XX, No. 2 (March 1975), p. 118.
10. Harold C. Edelstone and Ferne K. Kolodner, 'Are the Poor Capable of Planning for Themselves?' in Hans B. Speigel (ed.), *Citizen Participation in Urban Development*, Vol. I (National Training Laboratory Institute for Applied Behavioral Science, 1968), p. 240.
11. David M. Austin, 'Resident Participation: Political Mobilization and Organizational Cooptation,' *Public Administration Review*, Vol. XXXII No. 5 (September-October 1972), p. 413.
12. United Nations, *Popular Participation in Decision-Making for Development*, p. 17.
13. Sherry Arnstein, 'Eight Rings on the Ladder of Citizen Participation,' *Journal of the American Institute of Planners*, Vol. XXV No. 4 (July 1969), p. 217.
14. James Riedel, 'Citizen Participation: Myths and Realities,' *Public Administration Review*, Vol. XXXII No. 3 (May-June 1972), p. 216.
15. Phillip Selznick, *TVA and the Grass Roots* (New York: Harper and Row, 1966), p. 219.
16. Warren, Rose, Bergunder, p. 118; Elliott A. Krause, 'Functions of a Bureaucratic Ideology: Citizen Participation,' *Social Forces*, Vol. XVI, No. 2 (Fall 1968), p. 130.
17. John H. Strange, 'Citizen Participation in Community Action and Model Cities Programs,' *Public Administration Review*, Vol. XXXII, No. 5 (September-October 1972), p. 457.

18. Eugene Litwak, 'An Approach to Linkage in Grass Roots Community Organization' in Fred Cox *et al.* (eds.), *Strategies of Community Organization* (Itasca, Ill.: Peacock, 1974), Ch. 7, p. 134.
19. Arnstein, p. 216.
20. Reidel, p. 218.
21. Strange, p. 469.
22. Charles J. Grosser, 'Organizing in the White Community,' *Social Work*, Vol. XVI, No. 3 (July 1971), p. 26.
23. United Nations, *Popular Participation in Decision-Making for Development*, p. 61.
24. Nancy Runkle, Hooyman, *The Problem Definitions and World Views of Working Class Whites* (Doct. Diss., University of Michigan, 1974), p. 52.
25. Daniel Kramer, *Participatory Democracy* (Cambridge, Mass.: Schenkman, 1972), p. 133.
26. Hooyman, p. 278.
27. Warren, Rose, Bergunder, p. 127.
28. Bernard Barber, 'Participation and Mass Apathy,' in Alvin Gouldner (ed.), *Studies in Leadership* (New York: Russell and Russell, 1965), p. 477.
29. Everett M. Rogers and F. Floyd Shoemaker, *Communication of Innovations: A Cross Cultural Approach* (New York: The Free Press, 1971).
30. United Nations, *Popular Participation in Decision-Making for Development*, p. 61.
31. Robert Aleshire, 'Power to the People: An Assessment of the Community Action and Model Cities Experience,' *Public Administration Review*, Vol. XXXII No. 5 (September-October 1972), p. 438.
32. Frances F. Piven, 'Participation of Residents in Neighborhood Community Action Programs,' Speigel, Vol. I, p. 118.
33. Louis Harris, 'Report by the Senate Subcommittee on Intergovernmental Relations on Citizen Estrangement,' *Newsweek* (December 10, 1973), pp. 40-8.
34. Reidel, p. 213.
35. Lisa R. Peatie, 'Reflections on Advocacy Planning,' in Speigel, Vol. II, pp. 237-50.
36. Ibid., p. 237.
37. Piven, p. 119.
38. Irving Lazar, 'Which Citizens to Participate in What?' in Edgar Cahn and Barey A. Passett (eds.), *Citizen Participation: Effecting Community Change* (New York: Praeger, 1971), pp. 278-95.
39. Gary English, 'The Trouble with Community Action,' *Public Administration Review*, Vol. XXXII No. 3 (May-June 1972), p. 226.
40. Edelstone and Kolodner, p. 234.
41. United Nations, *Social Change and Social Development Policy in Latin America* (1970), p. 307.
42. Krause, p. 138.
43. United Nations, *Popular Participation in Decision-Making for Development*, p. 40.
44. Rogers, p. 35.
45. Piven, p. 125.
46. Litwak, 'An Approach to Linkage...,' p. 135.
47. Riedel, p. 216.
48. United Nations, *Popular Participation in Decision-Making for Development*, p. 55.

49. Selznick, p. 220.
50. Warren, Rose, Bergunder, p. 114.
51. Van Til, Van Til, p. 321.
52. Austin, p. 419.
53. Warren, Rose, Bergunder, p. 119.
54. Aleshire, p. 438.
55. *Social Change and Social Development Policy in Latin America*, p. 304.
56. Marjorie Mayo, 'Community Development: A Radical Alternative?' in Bailey and Brake, *Radical Social Work*, p. 132.
57. Ibid., p. 134.
58. Litwak, 'An Approach to Linkage. . .,' p. 136-7.
59. *Development and Participation: Operational Implications for Social Welfare*, Proceedings of the XVIIth International Conference on Social Welfare, p. 333.
60. Austin, p. 412.
61. Edlestone and Kolodner, p. 237.
62. United Nations, *Popular Participation in Decision-Making for Development*, p. 110.
63. Austin, p. 412.
64. Carl W. Stenberg, 'Citizen and the Administrative State: From Participation to Power,' *Public Administration Review*, Vol. XXXII No. 3 (May-June 1972), p. 193.
65. Michael Lipsky, 'Protest as a Political Resource,' *American Political Science Review*, Vol. LXII No. 4 (December 1968), p. 1150.
66. Cox, *et al.*, p. 223.
67. Eugene Litwak, 'Community Participation in Bureaucratic Organizations: Principles and Strategies,' *Interchange*, Vol. I., No. 4 (1970), p. 50.
68. Cox *et al.*, p. 411.
69. Ibid., p. 223.
70. Ibid., p. 398.
71. Robert Seaver, 'The Dilemma of Citizen Participation,' in Speigel, Vol. I, p. 70.
72. Peter Marris and Martin Rein, 'The Voice of the People,' in Speigel, Vol. I, p. 132.
73. United Nations, *Popular Participation in Decision-Making for Development*, p. 80.
74. Eugene Litwak: Josephena Figureria, 'Technological Innovation and Theoretical Functions of Primary Groups and Bureaucratic Structures,' *American Journal of Sociology*, 73:4 (January, 1968), p. 470.
75. United Nations, *Popular Participation in Decision-Making for Development*, p.84.
76. Grosser, *New Directions in Community Organization*, pp. 171-2.
77. Si Kahn, *How People Get Power* (New York: McGraw-Hill, 1970).
78. Litwak, 'An Approach to Linkage. . . ,' p. 134.
79. Kahn, *How People Get Power* (New York: McGraw-Hill, 1970).
80. Litwak, 'An Approach to Linkage . . . ,' p. 135.

Chapter IX
EDUCATIONAL POLICY AND PLANNING

1. *Sharing in Development: A Program of Employment, Equity and Growth for the Philippines.* Report of an Inter-Agency Team financed by the United Nations

Development Program and organized by the International Labor Office, 1974, pp. 337-340.

2. Phillip H. Coombs, *What is Educational Planning?* (Paris: United Nations Educational, Scientific and Cultural Organization; International Institute for Educational Planning, 1970), p. 2.

3. F. Harbison and C. A. Myers, *Education, Manpower and Economic Growth* (New York: McGraw-Hill, 1964).

4. Ralph Miller, 'The Meaning of Development and Its Educational Implications,' a paper prepared for a conference on education and development convened by the Canadian International Development Agency, Bellagio, Italy, May 1972.

Chapter X
EDUCATION FOR SOCIAL DEVELOPMENT

1. *Training Social Welfare Manpower* (New York: Council on Social Work Education, 1969), p. 31.

2. Dame Eileen Younghusband, 'Developing the Faculty: The Opportunities and Demands of Teaching' in Joseph Soffen (ed.), *The Social Work Educator* (New York: Council on Social Work Education, 1969), p. 29.

3. See Fred Riggs, *Administration in Developing Countries* (Boston: Houghton Mifflin, 1964).

4. For a discussion of this point see Irving A. Spergal, 'Social Development and Social Work,' *Administration in Social Work*, Vol. I, No. 3 (Fall 1977), pp. 221-33.

5. Jack Stumpf, 'Teaching an Integrated Approach to Social Work Practice' in Lilian Ripple (ed.), *Innovations in Teaching Social Work Practice* (New York: Council on Social Work Education, 1970).

6. *Proceedings of the International Conference of Ministers Responsible for Social Welfare* (New York: United Nations, September 1968, No. E. 69. IV. 4).

7. *Report of the First Asian Conference of Ministers Responsible for Social Welfare* (Manila, 1970).

8. *Problems and Prospects in Schools of Social Work Contributing to Development in the ECAFE Region* (Bangkok: United Nations, November 1972, No. E/CN. 11/SD/ Sem. SWT/L.3). The reference point of the seminar was David Drucker, *An Exploration of the Countries of Asia, with Special Reference to the Relevance of Social Work Education to Social Development Goals* (Bangkok: United Nations, 1972). Drucker's research was carried out during 1971 under the sponsorship of the Social Development Division of ECAFE and UNICEF (East Asia and Pakistan Region).

9. School of Social Service Administration, The University of Chicago, *Announcements*, Vol. LXXV, No. 1 (September 12, 1975), p. 31.

10. The School of Social Service Administration of the University of Chicago and the School of Social Service of St. Louis University.

11. The School of Social Development of the University of Minnesota, Duluth.

12. The term *community* development has sometimes been used interchangeably with social development, and at other times has been used to designate programs and processes somewhat narrower and/or more local in scope than

those described in this chapter. A useful listing of education and training programs in community development, encompassing programs of varying foci and scope, has been published in Lee J. Cary (ed.), *Directory: Community Development Education and Training Programs Throughout the World, 1976 Edition* (Columbia, Missouri: Community Development Society, 1976). Perusal of the *Directory* underscores the fact that social development and community development education programs have been generated and housed in a wide variety of academic and professional disciplines.

13. For general works on community organization techniques see, Fred M. Cox, *et al.* (eds.), *Strategies of Community Organization: A Book of Readings*, Second Edition (Itasca: Peacock, 1974); Ralph M. Kramer and Harry Specht, *Readings in Community Organization Practice* (Englewood Cliffs: Prentice-Hall, 1969); and Charles F. Grosser, *New Directions in Community Organization: From Enabling to Advocacy* (New York: Praeger, 1973).

14. See, for example, Carol H. Weiss, *Evaluating Action Programs: Readings in Social Action and Education* (Boston: Allyn and Bacon, 1972).

15. Thomas R. Dye, *Understanding Public Policy* (Englewood Cliffs: Prentice-Hall, 1972), pp. 23-4.

16. See, for example, Howard E. Freeman and Clarence C. Sherwood, *Social Research and Social Policy* (Englewood Cliffs: Prentice-Hall, 1970).

17. See John F. Jones and Rama S. Pandey, 'Social Development: Implications for Social Work Education,' *Social Development Issues*, Vol. 1, No. 3 (Winter 1978), pp. 40-54.

18. For a discussion of the significance and limitations of research relevant to social development, see Virginia A. Paraiso, 'Social Service in Latin America: Functions and Relationships to Development,' *Economic Bulletin for Latin America*, Vol. XI, No. 1 (April 1966).

19. See P. D. Kulkarni, 'The Developmental Function and Interdisciplinary Nature of Social Welfare,' in *Education for Social Change: Proceedings of the XVIIth International Congress of Schools of Social Work*, Nairobi, July 6-9, 1974 (New York: International Council on Social Welfare, 1975), p. 32.

20. In support of this assumption see Richard J. Estes and John S. Morgan, 'World Social Welfare Analysis: A Theoretical Model,' *International Social Work*, Vol. XIX, No. 2 (1976), pp. 3-15.

Index